FOR BARBARA,

FOR GEORGE, RECENTLY COME FROM GOD.

By a departing light

We see acuter, quite,

Than by a wick that stays.

There's something in the flight

That clarifies the sight.

And decks the rays.

-Emily Dickinson

By A Departing Light.

Foreword

Ian Jennings is not the first person to ask me to write a foreword for his book, and I doubt that he will be the last. I usually hedge my bets by saying, 'I'll give you a definite answer once I have seen the complete text," but with Ian I promised I would do it when he was still in the early stages of writing, and without seeing a single sentence of his work. We had never met face to face in any meaningful way: our closest personal encounter was at a diocesan conference where I was keynote speaker and he was among an audience of many hundreds. But I had accepted a friend request from him on Facebook, and followed his posts during the months when he was reflecting on his loss, and trusted my intuition that here was someone who was working through pain with integrity, and for whom the prism of faith was providing a life giving focus. I admired his openness and honesty, and now that his book is finished I have not been disappointed. Nor will you be. While the starting point was his wife, Barbara's untimely death, this is the story of a whole life and includes reflection on themes that will resonate with many – work/life balance, adoption, family coherence and spiritual resilience, retirement, de-cluttering and downsizing – all of them presented in an informed and inspirational way by a good storyteller.

At times of personal pain, we all have a tendency to be somewhat self-indulgent, and Ian manages to strike a balance about being honest and realistic about the challenges he has faced while having the ability to place them in a wider context of the struggle to be fully human and fully Christian. It will always be a particular challenge to watch a loved one in the final stages of their journey through this life, but Ian was also struggling with his own health issues at the time, not to mention questions about faith and the meaning and the impact it inevitably has on relationships with people – and with God. Where do miracles fit in? And guilt? And prayer? Not to mention Heaven, and divine guidance and a hundred and one other unspoken questions – unspoken because you're not quite sure what they are, but you know they are real.

This story is full of emotion and honest reflection in the best sense of the words. Expect to be caught up in its narrative as you read; it is powerful stuff while not being oppressive or dull, though I would dare you not to shed a tear as you read it. I know I did. There is no shortage of wisdom for those who may be coping with their own bereavements, but others will find plenty to think about as Ian combines pastoral reflection, theological exposition, Bible study and spiritual discipline into one hopeful vision of both the struggles and the possibilities of a life lived to the glory of God. Academics would classify all of this as 'reflective practice': knowing ourselves in the light of what we know of God through Christ and, in the process of doing so, being caught up into a vision that transcends us all. It would be hard to think of a more appropriate way of celebrating the life of Ian's beloved Barbara.

John Drane

John Drane is author of The Macdonaldisation of the Church (Darton Longman and Todd 2000) Do Christians know how to be Spiritual? (Darton Longan and Todd 2005) As well as 3 best selling books on the Bible that have been translated into 60 languages. For more than 20 years he has played a key role in ecumenical thinking on action on mission - Co-Chair of the Mission Theology Advisory Group of the Archbishops Council of the Church of England.

By a Departing Light

Can you believe what has happened to me?'

Barbara looked up at me from her iPhone with a bright eyed smile of triumph. "I was first female in my age category today," she said. Saturday morning was always Parkrun in Rother Valley Country Park. We so enjoyed doing that run together. There was an element of competitiveness between us although we tried to remind ourselves "it is a run not a race." I checked my email from Parkrun and discovered I was first male in my age category; however, I noticed I was the only male in my age category. I announced the former without mentioning the latter. She raised her eyebrows, head slightly tilted in interrogation, "Were you the only one?" She quizzed with a wry smile.

It was another thing we enjoyed doing together and we were looking forward to doing more of it in retirement. We had started running together a few years earlier, but soon discovered that running and talking did not work well. We could run or talk but we couldn't do both at the same time! The solution was simple: we ran in opposite directions around Rother Valley Lake and when we met in the middle of the route we did a high five! We were in countdown to retirement mode. We were looking forward to much more 'high fiving.' Only four months to go. All our plans were fully formed. We had a youthful sense of excitement.

It was a good day. We spent the day in our newly refurbished flat that was to be our home in retirement. I spent time quietly meditating on tomorrows sermon and Barbara was busy cleaning until the place shone with pristine splendour. We decided to stay that night as the beds were made up. The plan was to be up and off early on the Sunday back to the Rectory ready for a day of work and worship in the lovely Church of All Saints Aston where I was the Rector.

Around 4am Barbara complained of feeling sick and said, "I'm getting up, I'm feeling nauseous." As she got out of bed she added, "This feels different Ian, I haven't felt like this before." That worried me and I started to get up too. "Don't you get up," she said, "there's no point in both of us having a disturbed night." She wasn't actually sick but she began to feel very cold. Then she started to be confused. I sat directly in front of her, looked directly into her eyes and said, "you're really starting to worry me now Barbs." She smiled and said, "Yes it is worrying isn't it Matthew!" Matthew is our nephew so I realised with a sinking feeling that we were in trouble.

A phone call to Sarah was my next action. Sarah is our daughter and is always someone you would want to have around in a crisis. She was coming to the end of her nurse training. After my garbled explanation she said, "I'm on my way Dad, now ring the Health Service helpline." I was describing Barbara's symptoms when Sarah arrived. I was so relieved to see her. Almost immediately after Sarah arrived a new twist in the drama began to unfold. Barbara's eyes rolled back and she cried out with a sound somewhere between a scream and a groan. Her arms lifted in involuntary spasm and her whole body was wracked in a violent seizure. I was horrified to witness this happening to my Darling. Sarah took control. She had a cool head and her strength and skill came fully into play.

When the ambulance arrived the paramedics began working on Barbara. Her arms were flailing involuntarily so they could not get a line in to administer drugs. They decided to attempt to administer drugs rectally. This is the moment that Sarah wisely sent me out of the room. She pointed to the bedroom door and said, "Go in there Dad." I was happy to comply as this gave me an opportunity to pray – desperately, urgently.

I travelled with Barbara in the ambulance and the paramedics continued to work on her. Before we arrived at the Hospital she had suffered a further seven seizures. I prayed all the way. I thought I was losing her that day. Only two days earlier we had booked our flights for Switzerland for February 12th. Barbara's sister, Deborah had taught us both to ski. We were late starters and had acquired the most rudimentary of skills but we had been infected by our Swiss families enthusiasm and we were always trying to improve. We had been talking about it in the evening. We laughed together about the first time I hired skis. My younger brother in law, Gary had taken me to the ski supplier who said to me, "Have you been driving long?" "Yes' since I was seventeen," I replied, perplexed by the relevance of the question. "No, you really haven't," said Gary. "When he says driving he means skiing." Turning to the ski supplier I said, "This is the first time I have ever put skis on." I noticed that he then spoke to me slower and louder, "Well then, we will give you skis that will come off easily when you fall." That didn't immediately seem like a great idea so I said, "Why would I want skis that come off easily?" "Because," he added slower and slightly louder still, "if they do not come off when you tumble down the mountain side your ligaments can be twisted and torn and your bones can be broken." "Give me skis that will come off real easy," I pleaded. Barbara and I had laughed about that exchange on that Saturday evening as we planned another visit to the indoor ski centre in West Yorkshire to improve our skills before our trip. How life can change so completely and instantaneously.

Barbara was taken from the Emergency Room to the High Dependency Unit and was linked to life saving equipment. The family gathered around her bed. Our son Paul came with his wife Katie along with their two boys

Joseph and Jamie. Sarah went out to speak to Paul. She said, "Mum's very ill Paul." She looked up into his face as tears gathered at the corners of his eyes. We had already spoken with the Doctor. He didn't want to say more than that Barbara was very poorly. However Sarah asked the question, "Where is she on the Glasgow coma scale?" The Glasgow's Coma Scale is most commonly used to describe the level of consciousness in a person following a traumatic brain injury. The score goes from 3 to 15. Mild is 13 – 15; moderate is 9 – 12 and severe is 3 – 8. The Doctor said that Barbara was a 3. That's why Sarah felt the need to let Paul know just how serious it was. Barbara was put into a medically induced coma to stop the seizures and they began to treat her for encephalitis. This involved intravenous antibiotic and steroid medication.

Deborah and Gary flew in from Switzerland Barbara's sister, Pauline, and her husband cut short their holidays and returned from Italy and made their way home to be with her. My Sister Edith and her husband David came over from their home in Cleethorpes. I wrote in my diary on the Sunday evening of January 11th, "What a day the 11th turned out to be – My lovely wife so ill. I am in shock as I write this. All those violent, body wracking seizures and now in deep unconsciousness in Northern General ITU. God bring her back to me – please!"

The following day she did come back – confused, vulnerable, distressed but back. There was quite a crowd of us to welcome her when she emerged from her coma. We were allowed into the room two at a time. Barrier nursing was in force so we had to wear face masks. This increased her confusion. Sarah was last to come into the room. She was afraid of what she would find. She had witnessed the full vicious devastation of the seizures. She had seen her Mum become literally blue in the face and she worried that she might be permanently brain damaged because of the impact of the seizures. My younger sister-in-law, Emma took her for a coffee and was very supportive. So when she came into the room to see Barbs she was relieved that her Mum was back with us. After she left the room Barbara said to me, "Who was that?" I was shocked by this and there was a tremble in my voice when I said, "That was Sarah, our daughter." She repeated it loudly as if to inform the staff present in the room. I also detected a note of panic in her voice. She had lost so much so quickly and she had no idea why.

Barbara had huge difficulty in trying to process what had happened to her over the following few days. She said to everyone, "Can you believe what has happened to me?" Then she would add, "What has happened to me?" We went over the events time after time. She later confided that she felt really angry during those days. She woke up surrounded by the anxious faces of her family around her hospital bed and she had no memory of how she got there. She was angry that one moment she was remarkable healthy and the next her life was in jeopardy. "Everyone seemed pleased," she said, "and I couldn't understand why, there was nothing good about this." Life is precarious for all of us and there are some things for which you can make no preparation.

CHAPTER 2

Hanging onto Hope.

Preparation for retirement prompted many conversations. We were both well for our age; Barbara had always been punctilious about healthy lifestyle. She used to get slightly annoyed when people told her, "You are lucky to be so slim!" It was nothing to do with luck. She had worked at keeping herself fit and trim. As a student at college she had struggled with her weight; ice cream and butterscotch sauce was regularly on the menu in the college dining hall. She loved it. She talked about it for the rest of her life; her idea of food heaven.

We were married in the summer of 1972. Barbara was 21 and I was 25. She looked so beautiful in her wedding dress but she was irritated by her extra weight. Our first year of marriage was blissfully self-indulgent. We both worked hard and we both ate more than we should. Then we moved to South Wales where I became Pastor of a Church in Aberaman in the Cynon Valley. That move changed Barbara's life.

On our wedding day in July 1972 and our 40th Anniversary

It was a church with a strong and lively youth group. Barbara started a Sunday School Teachers' Training Class and a crowd of teenage girls attended. They would come to our home on Sunday afternoons for several months and she got to know them really well. Some were only a couple of years younger than she was. It just so happened that they were all slim and attractive. Barbara attributed the turning point in her own thinking to the influence of those girls, losing all her excess weight and committed herself to a life time of maintaining that weight loss. She never deviated from that determination.

On our 40th wedding anniversary Barbara, again, put on her wedding dress. She still looked beautiful but it was too big for her - she was slimmer at 61 than she had been at 21! But for her, it wasn't just about appearance, it was about healthy living. We walked together in the Peak

District every week. We were so committed to it that when we were so busy it looked like we would miss a week, we would get up at 4am and be out on the Peaks by 5 am. Seeing the sun come up over Stannage Edge together, made the effort worthwhile.

As we approached retirement we dared to hope for a long, healthy and happy time to share. We didn't have any of the age related ailments with which we had seen others struggle. I remember the conversation we had about old age and health agreeing that it was reasonable for us to expect to grow old together. We were not smug, we added the rider, "Unless incurable cancer is lurking around the corner." However, as the days advanced during Barbara's hospitalisation, we again began to hope for the future. She was diagnosed with encephalitis - an inflammation of the brain caused by infection. Although a very rare and serious condition we were assured that it was treatable and though it may take two years to fully recover, we could still look forward to enjoying retirement together.

However, one thing still nagged at us – in an almost throwaway remark one Doctor said, "there is just the remote possibility that it could be a brain tumour." Hearing that our son, Paul, was deeply unhappy. He worried, "why can't we have a definite diagnosis and if encephalitis is so rare how can the Doctors be so confident in proposing it as a diagnosis." Paul had just spent six years in the USA and his personal experience of medical diagnosis there was of thorough investigation that begins with the worst possible scenario and eliminates that before moving on to other possibilities. The encephalitis diagnosis persisted however; the Head of Neurology was convinced that this was correct. I recently found an entry in Barbara's diary for 11th January 2015, written a few weeks after the event which simply said, "Hospital 17 days – encephalitis – brain infection." The narrative was clear and oft repeated; she believed it.

During her time in Hospital, I visited Barbara every afternoon and evening, usually on my own in the evening. On the 26th of January, however, on the eve of her discharge from Hospital, Barbara complained to me that I never visited her alone. It bothered me that she had no memory of our evenings alone together; every day seemed like a blank sheet. She was hugely relieved to be discharged from Hospital but still in shock that she had suffered a brain trauma. She said, "I can't believe that this has taken away a bit of my brain power." At this stage we were still hoping that this loss would prove temporary.

Treatment continued upon discharge from Hospital. Three times a day medication was administered by means of a pic line. She had been released from Hospital on the understanding that Sarah would administer her Mum's medication. This involved three visits a day; 7 am; 1pm; and 9pm. Sarah was so happy to be able to do this for her

Mum even though it added significantly to her already busy schedule. Friends, family and colleagues came to visit Barbara during those days. She was always pleased to see them although she was easily tired. Pauls serious disquiet continued. "Dad," he said, "this might be a misdiagnosis."

Barbara was experiencing simple seizures after her release from Hospital. They consisted of what she described as a wave that came over her. It wasn't a violent seizure it just involved a momentary episode that left her feeling weaker. We were asked to record these episodes and we were told it was a matter of making adjustments to epilepsy medication. She was trying so hard to improve. She was daily pushing herself and testing her energy. We often went for coffee in the morning and she was usually keen to try a little walk in the Botanical Gardens afterwards. She would then be wiped out and need to go home to bed.

On February 9th we did our usual morning coffee and then Barbara suggested I take her for a little drive into Derbyshire. All the beauty of the Peak District was on our doorstep. I didn't go far. It was a bright and beautiful morning and the Mayfield Valley looked magnificent bathed in morning sunshine. Barbara was animated, much like her old self. I was so pleased to hear her talk with enthusiasm of the grandeur that surrounded us. In an instant that changed as the colour drained from her face. "Something is not right Ian," she said, "please take me home, I suddenly feel dreadful." I could see fear and dismay in her eyes. She told me later that she had thought she was dying. She was very ill throughout the night and the next day she stayed in bed. I wrote in my diary, "My Barbs is a very poorly girl! This is going to have to be a very slow journey of recovery."

That led to further conversation with the Neurologist who decided that Barbara needed to come back into Hospital. Barbara was actually relieved to be going back in. She said she knew it was the best move as she knew that all was not well, "I feel safer in Hospital," she said. We hoped that this stay would lead to adjustments to her medication that would lead to stabilisation of her condition. That seemed to happen to a degree because within the week she was back home and feeling positive again. I secured the use of a wheelchair and we started daily trips to nearby parks. She didn't always need the wheelchair but it was there when she did need it.

Within a few days we had a encouragingly positive appointment with Dr Price, the Head of Neurology. She said many affirming things that made Barbara feel very positive about the future. In fact that afternoon she talked to me about going swimming soon. Dr Price rang our home that same evening to say that the following day there was going to be a meeting of the whole team looking after Barbara to review her tests and CT scans. I asked the question, "How sure are you that this is encaphilitis, what percentage would you give it?" She replied, "I'm 99 percent certain." The next day she rang again; 99 percent had vanished to nothing. "I'm sorry to say that your wife's condition is not what I thought it was after all, she has a brain tumour and is being referred for surgery."

Paul had been right all along.

Yet hope continued to assert itself. Hope that is more than just wistful longing. The Psalmist writes that 'God delights in those who put their hope in his unfailing love.' (Psalm 147:11) That hope had informed and sustained our whole lives and we never needed it more than at that moment.

CHAPTER 3

Choose Life!

Barbara's appointment with the Neuro Surgeon took place on her 64th birthday. He confirmed that there was a tumour in her left temporal lobe and that he would operate within the next three weeks. The Surgeon's questions were endless but Barbara was surprisingly relaxed and at ease. Now that she knew what she was facing she felt she could face it. The Surgeon said it was eminently operable and was a small tumour. After the appointment we drove out to Curbar Edge in the Peak District and then on to Bakewell for a stroll along the river bank and something to eat. I was amazed by the contrast with the previous week. The week before all that Barbara had wanted to do was sleep and now she seemed to have some of her old vitality back.

I recently found this entry in her diary on the day after the appointment, "Well, here goes! I didn't have encephalitis but I do have a brain tumour. It is not aggressive. They are intending to operate within the next month as there is some preparation to do first. The surgeon said, 'This will be successful; you will come through this!'" The surgeon spelt out the dangers of course but his overall message was very positive. He leaned forward in his seat and said with a broad reassuring smile, "This is very amenable to surgery and is not aggressive." You do feel rather helpless in these situations and dependent upon the expertise of others. We were so grateful for this reassurance and clung to it. But it is characteristic of Barbara that she records this turn of events in a matter of fact way without hand wringing or self pity, "Well here goes!" It seemed to say, "Well, here is a turn of events that I would not have chosen but let's get on with it." That was her style.

Easter Day was April 5th. It was my final Sunday as Rector of All Saints. The Church was packed and to my surprise Paul, Katie, Joe and Jamie arrived from Harrogate to be present at my final service. Sarah was there too but Barbara was not quite well enough to cope with it. It was an emotional morning of course. It was a joy to serve these parishes for 9 years. We had learned together and laughed together. We had seen folks grow to maturity in faith. I had witnessed the development of our lovely, lively children from All Saints School; they and their parents a valued part of the church community. There was such care, compassion and warmth in this vibrant church family and it was hard for me to say goodbye. I preached on the radiant light of Easter and as I warmed to the theme light shone through the stained glass window directly on me. It was a magical moment which Sarah caught on camera. I told the people of Barbara's condition and forthcoming operation. I recounted the positivity of the surgeon and said, "We are looking forward to a summer of recovery."

Rev Ian Jennings' final service at Aston All Saints on Easter Sunday

Barbara's operation was scheduled for April 20th. I took her into operation admissions for 7am. She was first on the list which meant her operation was to take place at 8.30am. We were told to expect it to take four hours. Paul, Sarah and I went for a run whist Barbara was in surgery. We ran from our flat to Millhouses Park, through the Park and back home by a different route. It was about 5 miles. Every step was a prayer. When the phone rang we were told that the operation had gone well. When we saw Barbara she was very confused and not making sense but her first intelligible words to me were, "I'm alive!" It was said with a beaming smile.

Ten days later we sat in the office of the surgeon. His smile was reassuring and his opening comments disarming. "The operation was a success,' he said. We smiled and nodded and glanced at each other reassuringly. "I was able to remove the whole tumour," more smiles. "That's very good," I said. "Yes, it is," said the surgeon but I noticed a slight change of attitude, a lack of eye contact, a more measured tone. "When the tumour was examined under the microscope we discovered benign cells which is what we expected, but also pools of aggressive cells were present. Diffusion has occurred and it was established that you have Glioblastoma Multiform Grade Four. This is not good news I'm afraid." Barbara leaned forward with a broad smile and said, "But you're not telling me that I'm going to die, are you?" The directness of her question seemed to wrong foot the surgeon. "Oh no," he replied. "We're talking about living, not dying." The nurse who was also in the room added, "we have people with your condition who have been with us for seven years and are still doing well." That answer helped Barbara but alarmed me. I discovered later when I looked on line that GBM4, (as it is referred to) is a very aggressive cancer and that longevity is considered to be 18 months to 2 years.

Later that day we had a little walk together in the Botanical Gardens and Barbara was full of hope. "Seven years Ian," she said, picking up the words of the nurse. She said it as if seven years was a given, a minimum to expect. "Do you think I could live for ten years? I would so love to live for another ten years." She felt that since she had always been so fit and healthy that may help to give her a head start. Her face lit up at the thought. Then she added, "But I don't just want to exist, I want to live."

Lots of friends soon responded to Barbara's condition with promises of prayer. It was never trite or glib. It was a loving, God centred gift of prayer. Of course prayer is not an easy option or a simplistic solution. We love the neat narrative, the happy ending. How I would love to able to write, 'So everybody prayed and the tumour disappeared.' My friend, Peter Butt sent a simple message, "Praying for Barbara's complete healing." I valued that because I know him to be strong in faith and deeply prayerful. But prayer doesn't guarantee that things will resolve in the way we want.

"I never liked Jazz music because Jazz music does not resolve," wrote Donald Miller. He went on to say, "But I was outside the Baghdad Theatre in Portland one night when I saw a man playing the saxophone. I stood there for

15 minutes and he never opened his eyes. After that I liked Jazz music. Sometimes you have to watch somebody love something before you can love it yourself. It is as if they are showing you the way." Prayer is like that. If you want it to resolve neatly you might be disappointed but if you spend time around people who really love prayer you might discover that it is about being held in the affirming embrace of God's love. You might find it possible to live with questions, yet knowing, in the words of Mother Julian of Norwich, that "All will be well, all manner of things will be well." Sometimes 'you need someone to show you the way.' During the unfolding narrative of Barbara's illness prayer was hugely important.

Radiotherapy and Chemotherapy were on the agenda but before that began Barbara was keen to push herself. "Whatever of life remains," she said to me, "I must make the most of it." Looking back in my diary I am surprised to see how much walking we did during the month of May. The longest walk was to the Kings Oak half way round Derwent Reservoir. I had really forgotten what a lengthy walk it is. My plan was to walk to the tree, get Barbara settled on the bench and then I planned to jog back for the car and pick her up from there. However, after the third mile I realised I had miscalculated. The weather was closing in and the wind was getting strong. We pressed on to the Oak and my heart was in my mouth. It was 5 miles back to the car. Barbara was looking pale and tired and the weather was now cold, wet and windy. This was a moment for prayer. In my mind I said, "God, some help would be greatly appreciated right now!" At that moment a couple emerged from the woods and walked towards their car. They kindly responded to my request for a lift. It turned out that the lady was also recovering from a serious cancer operation and this little trip was part of her effort to recover. They were kind and lovely and they saved the day.

They were difficult days but Barbara's characteristic determination was in evidence and we walked daily. They were never the 10 – 15 miles hikes that we had been used to but walks in the Peak District that were short and wonder filled. We stood on Higgar Tor and held each other with tears as we drank in the beauty of God's creation; we walked along the river from Hope to Castelton and gazed at the grandeur of the surrounding Peaks observing also the lonesome pine on the ridge that we called, "our tree." I realised, looking back, that Barbara was pushing herself. She often came home from our walks in the late afternoon and went straight to bed and then slept until the next morning.

In the 1980s big baggy T shirts were popular that had a slogan emblazoned on the front. 'Choose Life,' was one of the most popular of these. That used to make me smile because it is actually a biblical text direct from the book of Deuteronomy. I'm sure most of the wearers thought it was a cool disco slogan but it was first the call of God to his people and in fact to the whole human family to 'choose life.' Barbara was always a life chooser and I could see that is what she was doing, consciously, daily, choosing life. Every morning she got out of bed, battled through this energy sapping disease and deliberately chose life.

CHAPTER 4

Panic, Prayer and Press-ups.

The Radiotherapy and Chemotherapy treatments began. As the Radio-Therapy treatment was delivered Barbara's head was held rigid in a mesh mound that had been made for her. She never complained - she just got on with it. Chemo Therapy sometimes caused vomiting and the worst of this brought her back into Hospital on a drip for 24 hours.

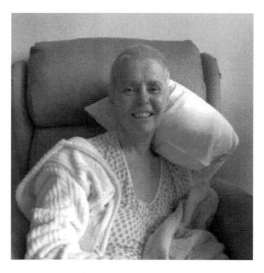

Barbara at Weston Park Hospital, receiving treatment

When we got up on the morning of June 27th she said, "I feel weird." I asked what she meant and she said, "More absent." Following this we had a tough few days and I awoke suddenly in the middle of the night, with a vivid sense of a very worrying future. I felt a rising sense of panic. I wanted to put on my trainers and run. I stood in our flat in the dark and felt the darkness closing in around me. The thought occurred that I could go out of our front door, stand on the landing and look over the city, but I knew I wouldn't want to return.

I decided on two strategies as a way to handle this panic-stricken paralysis; physical activity and spiritual activity – press-ups and prayer. Some years ago I read "God of Surprises" by Gerard Hughes. He developed the thought of 'breathing prayer.' He suggested breathing out self; everything that is harmful, negative and destructive and breathing in God – grace, love and mercy. He suggested not to be too cerebral about it; not to try to be too analytical but to develop it as a simple, spiritual exercise that is faith filled and God focused. So I breathed. Out – stress! In – trust! Out - fear – in – love! Out – self! In – Christ! I repeated these many times until a gentle rhythm was established.

Then at the end of each series of breathing prayers I quoted scripture verses. 'Trust in the Lord with all your heart and lean not on your own understanding; in all your ways acknowledge him and he will make your paths straight.' (Proverbs 3:6) 'Casting all your cares upon Him, for he cares for you.' (1 Peter 5:7)

Breathing in love must be accomplished by breathing out fear. 'There is no fear in love. But perfect love drives out fear.' (1 John 4:8) Expelling fear by opening up to God's love brings a deep spiritual balance. 'The love of God is poured into our hearts by the Holy Spirit whom he has given to us.' (Romans 5:5)

Exhaling self and inhaling Christ was also part of this spiritual exercise. The dark cell of ego is a narrow space and a life limiting place. So Galatians 2:20 sprang readily to mind, St. Paul writes, 'I have been crucified with Christ and I no longer live, but Christ lives in me. The life I live in the body I live by the faith of the Son of God, who loved me and gave himself for me.' Also, 'Christ in me the hope of glory.' Shifting the central basis of your life from self to Christ is a liberating experience. It lets the light shine in.

That made me remember Brad (not his real name) who was a young prisoner in Doncaster prison when I was the Anglican Chaplain there. Brad came to faith in prison, never missing a chapel service or group. He was determined not to return to his offending pattern of behaviour and was keen to grow in his new found faith. One Sunday morning I came into the prison and he was waiting for me at the Chapel door. I'd no idea how he got there as there was another hour before the service was due to start and prisoner movement wasn't allowed. "Oh Father Ian," he said, "I'm so glad to see you, I had a terrible dream last night." "What was your dream Brad?" I asked. His reply amused me, "I dreamed I was in prison," he said. I laughed and said, "Then you woke up and found your dream had become true!" "No!" He said, "You don't understand, I was really in prison! It was horrifying. I was broken and defeated. I was in despair but then I woke up and found I was free!" "How's that?" I asked. "I'm free inside," he said touching his heart, "God loves me, he has forgiven and accepted me and my future is going to be different from my past.' He had a new radiance. It was an epiphany moment for him and the light had shone in.

I thought of him in the middle of that's desperate night. His experience did not change as he was still in prison but the prison wasn't in him. I needed the light to shine in so that the darkness did not overwhelm me.

When I had finished the prayers I then started on press-ups and pushed my elderly frame until I was quite exhausted and ready for sleep. Barbara was oblivious to these events and her steady breathing continued as I crawled back into bed.

That pattern of prayer became part of my daily routine. Sarah would come and sit with her Mum so that I could run. Running and breathing go rather well together! This style of prayer links perfectly with the rhythm of running. I also included some set prayers like the Lord's Prayer and the Collect for Purity at the Eucharist along with the Gloria. I also included brief urgent intercessions. I knew that if my prayers were wholly extemporaneous, eventually they would narrow down to one thought only, a desperate, wailing plea for Barbara's healing repeated ad infinitum. Prayers for Barbara were part of my daily prayer but not my exclusive focus, as my prayer life would have ground to a halt as she continued to deteriorate.

Barbara was always pleased to hear that people were praying for her. One day an envelope was posted through our door which contained a card and a hanky. It was from Healing Rooms, an organisation that I had heard a little about; a national movement of people who pray for healing. They are a multi denomination group meeting on a weekly basis. We had no idea how they had come to know of Barbara's condition, it came out of the blue. Barbs put the hanky on her head, under her woolly hat. She was delighted laughing about it all day. She wasn't cynical but glad that people were thinking of her in prayer. She welcomed it and wouldn't take it off. That night, when she went to bed she said, "That has made me feel better all day today." She valued prayer although she did not think we could twist God's arm for a miracle. Prayer so often brought whispers of love, rumours of angels and hints of Heaven. Our miracle was, despite the tragedy of terminal brain cancer she fought to live. Her light still shone brightly each day.

When Barbara became ill she was unable to focus on reading. She had taught A level English Literature, loved books and inspired others to love reading but, sadly, never read another book. The tumour took that – and so much else – away from her. I watched her diminishing capabilities daily and was frightened. One day she said to me, "What's your name?" I was shocked. I said, "I'm Ian, your husband." She said, "Where do you live?" I replied, "I live here with you, we've been married 44 years." "Where do you sleep?" "I sleep in that bedroom with you, but you knew all that didn't you Barbs?" She looked anxious as she hesitatingly said, "Yes but things might have changed." My lovely wife was changing; disappearing before my eyes. I woke up afraid every morning. Prayer helped to manage that, but it could not eliminate it.

My friend Warwick Shenton died as a result of a brain tumour; he had been experiencing headaches and his GP had given him strong pain killers. He was an outstanding Christian Leader and was in demand as a speaker at Churches and Conferences. Whilst on a ministry trip to the USA the headaches worsened so his colleague took him to see a consultant who immediately ordered a scan with the result was that Warwick was told to fly straight home. He had a brain tumour which needed immediate surgery. Within days he was back home and being prepared for surgery. He came round from the operation long enough to squeeze his wife's hand but then suffered a catastrophic bleed to the brain and he never recovered consciousness. He was 54. His wife, Cynthia was devastated and broken hearted. When I asked her about dealing with grief she quoted from C.S.Lewis from 'A Grief Observed.' "No one ever told me that grief felt so much like fear."

That night of panic made me realise I was experiencing fear and I was already experiencing grief. I was losing my love.

CHAPTER 5

Confused and Distressed.

I was unfamiliar with the word 'Confabulation" but after the seizures Barbara was talking and making no sense. The Doctors said this was confabulation; something we learned a lot about during the remaining months of Barbara's life. It is defined as the production of fabricated, distorted and misinterpreted memories about oneself and the world, but without any conscious intention to deceive. Sometimes it could be quite bizarre. In the family we often had to say, "it's the tumour talking."

When Sarah called to see us Barbara would say, "Who's looking after your baby?" Sarah would respond, "Mum, I don't have a baby." Barbara would be genuinely surprised and continue to be concerned about the welfare of this imaginary baby.

Sometimes her vivid dreams were more real than the true events of the day. One morning she awoke angry and said to me, angrily, "I can't believe what you have been doing." I said, "What do you mean? What have I done?" She was furious, "You know exactly what you've been doing. Seven women!!" She repeated this with a strong downward gesture towards the bed. "Seven women in my bed!" My protestations of innocence fell on deaf ears. "You know it's true," she said with a look of disgust and disdain in my direction. "Don't you ever speak to me again!" I hoped she might have forgotten this in half an hour or so, as she did with so many things but this false memory fastened itself upon her deep consciousness. She took of her wedding ring and would give me no eye contact. When I called her 'Sweetheart' or 'Darling' she said, "Don't you ever call me by those names – never again."

When a teaching colleague from school came to visit Barbara she said, "I suppose everyone in school knows what he's been up to by now!" Her friend was completely non plussed. On occasions I asked Barbara when she thought I had entertained all these women since we had never been apart but by now she was beyond the point of clear and rational thought. Only Sarah's insistence, repeatedly telling her Mum that it wasn't real that finally convinced her. "Mum" she would say, "It didn't happen. It is just something that you dreamed." Eventually we had a lovely moment of reconciliation, she put her wedding ring back on and we hugged. It was actually a very precious moment. I felt I'd got my sweetheart back; at least for a while.

Barbara's cancer was in her left temporal lobe which plays a key role in speech, comprehension and verbal memory. Visual perception can also be damaged by left temporal lobe tumour. There were times that Barbara could see things that weren't there. There was a glass panel above our bedroom door upon which, she claimed, were words written in the glass. She said it was very beautiful calligraphy and asked if I could read it. She couldn't accept that it wasn't there and sometimes would draw visitors' attention to it.

Her most obvious difficulty was with words but she found alternatives when the right word would not come. Whilst she was in the Royal Hallamshire Hospital the Doctor said, "Do you know where you are Barbara?" She thought for a moment and then said, "The yellow embankment." She said it slowly and emphatically. The Doctor was bewildered, as I was myself. On reflection later, however, I realised what she meant. In front of the Hospital is an embankment and in the spring it is covered with daffodils. We had often driven past it and commented on how beautiful it looked. She couldn't remember the name of the building, but she remembered its most stunning visual feature. I thought it was a wonderfully imaginative explanation.

The "Yellow Embankment" outside the Royal Hallamshire Hospital

Sarah was very good at interpreting her Mums words. When Barbara said to the nurse, "Can I have my remote bangay and dopla?" Of course the nurse had no idea what she meant and turned to Sarah who said, "She wants her toothbrush and toothpaste." She was right. "However did you know that?" Asked the nurse. "I know my Mum," was Sarah's reply.

One of the worst aspects of Barbara's illness was the changes that took place in her understanding and behaviour as the disease advanced. It is the hardest thing to write about and at times, it was utterly terrifying. It was like fast track Alzheimers. She was distressed and anxious and sometimes quite paranoid. She could say things that were upsetting and completely out of character. We had to expect the unexpected and try to enter into her rapidly changing world. Our children were great with their Mum;

wise, caring, loving and cool and capable in a crisis. Love kept the wheels turning.

There were moments of clarity too. Like the moment Barbara woke up in the middle of a sunny afternoon, looked at me with a warm smile and said, "I do love you Ian." Only a short while before Sarah had come specifically to persuade her to take her medication. She had been refusing to take it for over 3 hours. It seemed that she put her deterioration down to the medication and since I was the one who gave that to her, I must be directly implicated – "I can't believe you have done this to me!" she had said. But now a moment of clarity and love -her broad sunny smile and words that were music to my ears, "I do love you Ian." So, so welcome.

One day she was upset because of her continued loss of mobility. "I can't climb stairs now. I won't be able to put the children to bed." Needless to say it has been 30 years or more since we needed to put children to bed. Later that same day she shouted me into the bedroom and said, "The sauce in Mum's wardrobe needs to be taken out and put into the ranchoo." It made no sense and I couldn't find a clue to what she meant but she repeated it with strong and clear emphasis, adding, "Show me the stones!" Her voice was loud and strong, clearly annoyed with me for my lack of comprehension. I was holding a basket of washing I had just taken from the drier which I showed her, "I think you mean this. I just got these from the drier."

That just made her so angry, she was out of bed in a flash, picking up the keys and heading through the front door on to the landing of our apartment building. "What's the answer?" She demanded. "Unless you tell me I'm going." Alarmed I said, "Going where?" "I'm leaving," she added moving towards the stairs to go down into the street. She was so vulnerable; she was trembling and seemed so tiny. I was desperately worried and used all my powers of persuasion to cajole her back inside. Finally she heeded my pleading promise to do better and she came back in. Within five minutes she had forgotten about it but events like that were frequent occurrences.

Our daughter, Sarah brought me a book called *Connections through Compassion*. It was a book of guidance for families and friends of brain cancer patients. It was written by two women, Joni Aldrich and Nysa Peterson, both of whose husbands had died of brain cancer. One of the things I found helpful was their advice, "Meet your loved one in their world. Impossible? Not as impossible as it may be for them to return to yours. Identify where he or she is today, and try to find joy with them there." So that is what I tried to do. It was far from easy but even on the darkest of days there were still moments of joy.

CHAPTER 6

Miracle and Mystery.

At 16 I was involved in a motor car accident; it was before the days of seatbelts. I was sitting in the front passenger seat and was projected through the windscreen of the car. My scalp was lacerated and my skull was fractured, but that mended just fine. The lasting legacy, however, was recurring back problems over the years. During a particularly painful phase a friend recommended I should see a chiropractor. I attended my appointment doubled up with pain. The receptionist directed me to the treatment room where I lay on the table in my underwear. The chiropractor walked in, a big muscular Australian who greeted me by saying, "So you're a Reverend are you? I suppose that means you believe in miracles?" He interlaced his fingers thrust downward and his knuckles cracked loudly. He then flexed his fingers and said, a challenging note in his voice, "So tell me about one miracle you have witnessed!" There was a challenging note in his voice. Lying there in agony in my underpants was not the most conducive moment for a debate so I quoted Albert Einstein, "For some people nothing is a miracle whilst for others everything is a miracle." I said I belong to the 2nd category. I see God in everything even in his skilled fingers, "I'm hoping for a little miracle for my back today." He harrumphed loudly and got to work.

I left feeling I had fluffed the moment of encounter, but also with considerable relief from my pain; that was miracle enough for me. I guess Einstein was commenting on living with a sense of wonder, encountering mystery and having ones eyes open to the extraordinary beauty and amazing complexity of the universe. Having God at the centre of life adds to the splendour, enhances the mystery and fills the heart with wonder.

If our meeting had been more conducive, I might have told my Australian friend about the time I was suffering intense stomach pain, recurring and increasing over a period of months. I consulted my GP who made an appointment with the Hospital for investigation. Easter intervened, and in those days the church where I was minister had an Easter Convention and we entertained two guest preachers, David Skelton and Bruce Millar, over a long weekend. They were both lively, faith inspiring preachers. On the Saturday morning the three of us went for a walk. At the top of Prestatyn High Street, the pain suddenly came. I was literally immobilised by it. I groaned, "I've got to find a chemist to get something for this pain." They both replied, "No we'll pray for you." "What? Now?" "Well of course," was their response. I tried to shrink into a doorway but they laid hands on my head and prayed for me in the street. To be honest I had no expectation of anything happening but as they finished their prayer, my pain faded away completely. It never came back. 42 years later, it still hasn't.

I attended the Hospital appointment after Easter and forgot about it. Weeks later my GP bumped into me in the street and said, "O, I forgot to let you know the results of your tests. They discovered you'd had a duodenal ulcer but it has healed up on its own. Only the scar remains - no further action is needed." I laughed and said, "Wow that's amazing." I told him what had happened at Easter. He smiled, "Well sometimes prayer works better than prescriptions" I did think it was extraordinary and that divine intervention seemed the only explanation. People of faith would have no difficulty in agreeing with that conclusion, yet most would agree that such events are rare. It is the daily encounter with the numinous which gives us a sense of the miracle of the moment, if we are open to it. Barbara and I endlessly talked theology. She was RE and English trained, but Divinity was her first subject. She was constantly curious and questioning, always in interrogatory mode. She was interested in people and hungry for fresh information. If we encountered a friend unexpectedly, her face would light up and she would launch into questions – their life, their family, their work, and their plans. I often came away thinking, "We know so much more about them but they know virtually nothing more about us." They didn't get chance to ask!

I did love that side of her character; she had studied theology at Lincoln and her questions were endless. We discussed matters of faith and dogma through 44 years of married life. As time went by she became more content to live with questions, rather than settle for trite conclusions. Barbara liked what the former Bishop of Blackburn said when terminally ill with cancer. He was asked whether the diagnosis had affected his faith. He replied by saying, "I now believe more and more about less and less." his faith in the great truth of God's never failing love remained as strong as ever and was growing stronger but the peripheral questions he left hanging in the air. So did Barbs.

Howard Clinebell suggests that, "We live in a period when it's not easy to find genuine religious answers. Contemporary religion in the West has lost much of the sense of the numinous and the transcendent. Many contemporary religious expressions are pale, and anaemic and lack the ecstatic, the mystery, the numinous." Barbara and I encountered the numinous; the sense of the transcendent; the awesome majesty and beauty of God. We opened our eyes and hearts to the glory of God. Sometimes in Church and sometimes in God's natural world. Our sense of God was just as real in the Peak District on a Monday as it was in All Saints Church on a

Sunday. Flying over the Alps one day we were both looking out of the plane window. No words passed between us but we held each other close and wept, silently, for the awesome beauty of God's creation. We felt Elizabeth Barrett Browning had a vision of God that rang true for us, ..."nothing's small,' she wrote, ..."but finds some coupling with the spinning stars." She goes on to say in those famous lines, "Earth's crammed with Heaven, and every common bush afire with God; But only he who sees takes off his shoes."

Barbara was impatient with religious pretentiousness and abhorred posturing super-spirituality. I was recently invited to speak at the end of term Full School Assembly at Barbara's school where she taught for 23 years. I was greeted so warmly by her former colleagues. One said, "I loved your wife. By the way she could be very irreverent and was least like a Vicar's wife of any Vicar's wife that I've ever known!" That was a great compliment. She was always fun-loving and outrageous. Her Christianity was never bristling, caustic or judgmental but rather warm, winsome and understated.

Seeing God in everything is not always easy. Life can be heavy and heartbreaking at times. I remember when Rev Dr Paul Walker addressed an assembly of Christian Ministers and recounted the tragedy of the death of his own son. His son had followed his Father's footsteps into the ministry. He was a very gifted young man and had completed his studies and was about to take up his first church appointment. He was driving very early on a Sunday morning to the church to lead the service for the first time and to commence his ministry. There was hardly any traffic on the road except, as it turned out, for one car, heading the wrong way – southbound in a northbound lane because the driver was very drunk. He hit the young minister head on and he was instantly killed.

Although it had happened some years earlier as he addressed the ministers gathering we could still sense the pain in his heart and hear it in his voice. The question was asked, "How can you see God in that event?" He replied with simplicity and honesty, "I don't see God in that event; it was a random event that could happen to anyone. Tragedy; disaster; accident; sickness – these are things that can befall anyone of us. We are not exempt."

I was pleased to hear his explanation - that through the searing pain of grief God had drawn very close to his wife and himself. He felt held by Love and sustained by Grace. I have heard people engaging in verbal dexterity and theological gymnastics to identify God's will in the midst of appalling tragedy; arguing that's it is all in God's plan and wrapping it up with sugar coated verses. It doesn't work. It is bad theology and bad pastoral practice.

Gaby Doherty wrote the book 'Grenfell Hope' following the Grenfell Tower fire. On that terrible night June 14th 2017 she watched, horror-struck from her bedroom window just two hundred yards away from the burning tower. Her husband, an Anglican Minister, went out to help. He along with many others reached out to the hurting, comforted the bereaved in their grief and sat with those who wept in their distress. Over the weeks that followed Gaby helped her own four children to process their trauma as well as reaching out to others. She writes, "I am glad about the choices I made. I chose to spend time with my friends. I chose to care for those around me … When life deals you a bad hand; you will also have to make choices. God can fuel you, or you can forget him and blame him for the things that have gone wrong. I chose to submit and be submerged in him. I prayed. I looked for purpose in everything … I tried to keep myself functioning, loving and healthy." It is hard to 'find purpose in everything' living the shadow of a burnt out tower and with over 70 dead. You simply can't see God in that but you can see him in the community coming together in love and care for the hurting and broken. You can see purpose in the outpouring of generosity. In the experience of grief, when you choose the path of love you find the path of purpose.

One question Barbara never asked when she knew the grim truth about her terminal diagnosis was, "Why me?" She had many questions about the nature of the disease and insisted that I research it on the web. I was reluctant to tell her what I had read as it was so awful, but she was determined to know as much as possible. "How are Paul, Katie, Sarah and the boys going to cope as I lose my intelligence?" She asked with tears as we stood in the kitchen and held each other.

When she was admitted to St Luke's Hospice for the first time she was very confused. The Doctor said to her, "Barbara do you know where you are?" She had no idea where she was but refused to be wrong footed. She thought for a moment and replied, "That's a very interesting question. Perhaps I could respond by asking you how many times you have asked that question today?" The Doctor looked flummoxed! I think it was a new experience for him. It was Barbara's attempt to stay in control by being the questioner rather than the questioned.

Barbara's questions kept coming and they were often heart breaking, "Ian where has the other half of me gone?" She was aware of losing capacity; aware of her diminishment. One morning, she said plaintively, "My throne is broken, isn't it Ian?" That seems like a strange comment but it spoke volumes to me. "My throne" the place of control, of rulership. Her control over decisions, actions and thoughts was slipping away. Her throne was broken.

CHAPTER 7
By a Departing Light.

Barbara was 65 when she died. I couldn't bring myself to use the phrase, 'She lost her battle with cancer.' Her illness did not defeat her and it did not define her; she won the battle of life. She had 65 years of joyous and vibrant living. St. Jerome said, 'The glory of God is the human person fully alive.' She was always fully alive.

We met when she was 17 and I was 21. We were both attending a Christian Conference in Clacton, in Butlins Holiday Camp. About 6000 Christians took over the whole place for a week. I was with my friend John Cox when we met a crowd of young people. "I know these," he said, "I'll introduce you." Barbara was one of them. She stood out from the crowd, so vivacious and vibrant - personality shone with a kind of radiant vitality and I couldn't help noticing that she was also very pretty. I said to myself, "here is someone I could fall in love with." It was a very brief meeting because it was the final day of the Conference but we met again one month later.

Barbara at the age of 17

Barbara's Dad was a Church planter, conducting a mission in Holmfirth with a view to establishing an infant church. My sister and brother in law lived there and I learned that he was staying in their home. I asked a few questions, with a feigned air of nonchalance, and discovered that there was to be an inaugural meeting of the new church and Barbara was coming to help with catering. Needless to say I contrived to be present. From my sister's home we travelled to the venue in the back of her Dad's car. This was the moment I chose - tentatively - to reach out for her hand. As our fingers touched she jumped, almost giving the game away. I was gratified to note that she did not move her hand. Our hands clasped and she shot me a reassuring smile. It was a wonderful moment. Our journey together had begun.

Later that year I began my studies training for the Ministry. I placed a picture of Barbara on my bedside cabinet. There were 6 other students in that room and when they knew she was only 17, they ribbed me mercilessly. "You mean you are going out with a school girl? You cradle snatcher!" Four years seems like an enormous age gap at that stage of life. Later it seems like nothing. Throughout our marriage Barbara used to joke, "As you can see I am married to a much older man!"

She was remarkably mature for 17. When we first met I discovered that she had a sister of 15, Pauline, and then a big gap to her sister, Deborah, who was two and a brother, John, aged one. Barbara absolutely loved her younger siblings and she was a great help to her Mum in caring for them. Early in our relationship I remember thinking, "This girl is an archetypal Mother." I couldn't imagine her being without children in her life.

I soon discovered that she was also a teacher in the making. I was staying with the family for a weekend and went with Barbara to the Sunday School. Barbara was the Sunday School Superintendent; I was genuinely amazed. It was quite a large Sunday School with classes in every age group and a staff of mature teachers. There was Barbara out at the front orchestrating the whole thing. I was so impressed by her confidence and capability; she was extraordinarily good at what she was doing. I recognised the teacher in her that day. She didn't choose to teach; teaching chose her. She always knew it.

She was junior/secondary trained and her first post was in a junior school in Doncaster. She worked really hard and teaching was never far from her thoughts. One night I came to bed late and she was already fast asleep. I didn't switch the light on and so stubbed my toe on the bed. Instantly Barbara sat up and in a loud voice said, "Right class eight! Shall we do some work!"

Her first teaching post in a secondary school was in Prestatyn. We moved there in June of 1975. There was a post advertised in the English department and Barbara applied and was duly appointed. During the summer holidays the head of English, came to see her at home. He said, "I want you to teach 'A' level English Literature from September." Barbs was shocked. "I don't think I can," she said. "I have only ever taught in junior school before." He was reassuring. "Don't worry, you'll be fine," he said. As soon as he left Barbara burst into tears and said, "I really can't do it Ian, I haven't got the skills." I said, "Barbs you can do this. How hard can it be? All you need is to be one step ahead of your students." Her summer was spent reading, planning, preparing so that she was never just one step ahead. She mastered her subject and relished the task.

During a lengthy teaching career she never lost her enthusiasm. In 1988 we moved from Birmingham to Sheffield. Barbara had taught in a tough inner city school in Birmingham. She then took up an English post in Wales High School in South Yorkshire. The contrast was vivid! She told me that during those early days she couldn't conceal the joy she found in teaching at Wales. She would come into the staff room at break time and wax lyrical about how easy it was to teach there. "The discipline is good, the children are so attentive and eager to learn – it's so easy," she declared with characteristic enthusiasm. She said to me later, "I realised I needed to shut up about it because I was really irritating some staff who didn't think it was easy at all." She learned to subdue her natural enthusiasm so as not to alienate her colleagues.

Ecclesiastes 9:10 says, "Whatever your hand finds to do, do it with all your might." In other words, whatever opportunities life presents to you, embrace them with enthusiasm. Seize life! Barbara did just that. Eugene Peterson translates those words, "Whatever turns up, grab it and do it. And heartily." That really does describe Barbara's approach to life. She became an outstanding year head. Her colleague told me that when Barbara stood up at Assembly, silence would fall. She worked at that. I was moved when Lisa, who took over from her as head of year when she retired, confided, "Barbs was my mentor, I loved her. I wanted to be her." Lisa has since become an outstanding Deputy Headteacher of the school and it is gratifying for me to know that my Barbs played a little part in the development of her career.

She was the oldest female teacher in her school by the time she retired. She came home one day and told me this little incident which highly amused her. Two boys were misbehaving in the corridor; she dealt with them swiftly and unerringly! As they walked away, somewhat subdued, another member of staff heard one say to the other, "Why is she still here? I thought they were made to retire at 70!"

Barbara loved poetry and one of her favourite poems was 'By a Departing Light' by Emily Dickerson. It is short but has extraordinary depth of meaning and beauty of construction:

By a departing light

We see acuter, quite,

Than by a wick that stays.

There's something in the flight

That clarifies the sight.

And decks the rays.

There was a bright radiance about Barbara's life. She never wanted to be the 'wick that stays' flickering, guttering and inching tortuously towards the end. When she knew her diagnosis was terminal she confided in me, "Ian I want to live as fully as I can, then leave as quickly as I can." We don't get to make that choice but she was never afraid of dying. She was heartbroken to be leaving us. One day, when we knew there was only a few months left, we hugged one another as we stood in the kitchen. She said, with tears, " I can't believe I have to leave you in a few months." A few days later when I was struggling with my emotions she said, "But dying is all right, isn't it Ian?" I said, "Yes, of course I just wish you didn't have to do it for a good while yet." My feeling is, that once she accepted the inevitability of her own death, she just wanted to get on with the process. She told people who loved her not to visit her. "Go and get on with your own life," she said. That was hard for them but I think she said it for two reasons; firstly because she was losing cognitive skills and her mental diminishment made conversation increasingly difficult; secondly she didn't want to be reminded of the richly rewarding lives of others when her own life was leaching rapidly away.

In 2016 I was diagnosed with Prostate Cancer and needed radical surgery. On May 11th I sat by Barbara's bed and held her hands. "I won't be able to visit you for a little while," I said, "I'm going into hospital for surgery tomorrow." She listened and concentrated so hard to understand. She looked so little and vulnerable. "I'm going to miss you," I said. "I'm going to miss you too," Barbara replied. I said, "I love you." "I love you too," then she added with a girlish smile, "you're so good looking!" That amused me. It took me back to when she was 17. "And you're very beautiful," I said. She was and always will be to me – my beautiful Barbs who won the battle of life.

CHAPTER 8

Grief and Guilt

In her very famous book, *On Death and Dying*, Elisabeth Kubler-Ross outlines five stages of grief. They are:

1. Denial and isolation
2. Anger
3. Bargaining
4. Depression
5. Acceptance.

She claims that these are universal and experienced by all cultures and people. There is no set time that we spend at each stage and we often move between stages before coming to a peaceful acceptance of the death of our loved one. Speaking personally, I think there are days since Barbara's death when I have experienced every stage within a single day. Everyone's journey of grief is different but I imagine that this is quite common.

Feelings of guilt are not given as a category, yet after speaking to many bereaved people; it seems that a sense of guilt is a common experience. Sometimes it is associated with anger. Anger is often directed towards the person who has died. Or perhaps it is a feeling of outrage, of having been left and your partner has gone, which lies behind the anger. It is completely irrational of course, but nevertheless is a genuine part of grief. I asked a friend, whose husband had recently died, how she was coping. She said, "It's so hard without him," and then she added with a wry smile, "But I could kill him for dying." For some the feeling of anger is profound and the accompanying feeling of guilt is equally strong. Every bereaved person experiences grief in a different way.

My own feelings of guilt arose from not being able to look after Barbara at home till the end of her life. In her final few months she was cared for in the Hospice or Nursing Home. Exactly one year after the first seizures took her into Hospital; more seizures took her back to Hospital. She came home after a couple of weeks, but it was clear that her condition had significantly deteriorated. It was from then that we knew she only had months left to live.

The Doctor came to see her at home. Her mental capacity was seriously compromised. Sarah sat next to her Mum on the sofa while the Doctor was examining Barbs and she couldn't hold back the tears. When Sarah was small she used to cry silently. Tears would flow soundlessly down her cheeks. This was yet another day of silent tears; there were many.

That day Barbara's behaviour had become more bizarre. She had smilingly kissed the kitchen work surface several times. When she opened her mouth to speak no words came out only unintelligible noises, spoken with expression as if she thought she thought she was forming intelligent sentences. It was heart breaking. The Doctor said, "I think Barbara needs to go into St. Luke's Hospice if they have a bed." He made a phone call and discovered a bed was available for the following day.

Barbara was awake and up at seven the following morning and said, to my surprise, "What time are we going?" I was amazed and delighted. "`Eleven o'clock," I replied. She got up and with a bit of help from me she showered and dressed. Sarah came at 10.30 to travel with us the two miles to St. Luke's. By this time Barbara was fully dressed and ready to leave. All at once the full import of this moment seemed to dawn on her and she picked up the hand towel and began furiously cleaning the bathroom sink. "We need to leave now," I said. She replied, "No! I need to clean this bathroom." It was hard to persuade her to give up cleaning and step out of the front door. We finally got into the car and set off. "Take me to the shops," she pleaded with agitation, "there are things I need." Of course she needed nothing but she was just so reluctant to arrive at St. Luke's. Later, she confided in Sarah that she knew that she would probably never go home again. She never did.

After her death I hated that bathroom. Every time I went in, the distressing image of her desperately cleaning the sink and polishing the taps for the last time haunted my mind. As I showered I would look through the glass doors at the sink and my tears would mingle with the shower water and I would be surprised by the volume of my own voice as I cried for my love. My guilt and grief mingled together: a stain the shower couldn't wash away.

St. Luke's Hospice in Sheffield is an extraordinary place. Its ethos breathes life - an odd comment when so many people there receive 'end of life care.' There is a depth of humanity and warmth of loving kindness in every member of staff. I was so impressed with the care Barbara received from everyone; the ancillary staff; the nurses; the catering staff; the chaplaincy team; the consultants and the support staff. All seem to share the same vision. No one is patronised; all are treated with a respect for value and dignity of every human life.

In many ways those early days at St. Luke's were very precious to us. I would come after breakfast each day and stay all day. Our little routine included a short walk in the grounds each morning for as long as Barbara could manage it and lunch together in the dining room, which included three extraordinarily good courses. Barbara was taking strong steroids which made her constantly hungry; it was just so nice to see her really enjoying her food. In the afternoon we would spoon together on her bed and sleep, our arms around each other. She often said, "Oh Ian, you have no idea how secure this makes me feel." Having Barbs in the Hospice brought me a great deal of relief personally. There had been many terrible nights before Barbara was admitted to St. Luke's. One night she awoke me coughing and choking. She had taken the top of the talcum powder and was trying to ingest it. "How do they expect me to get this stuff down?" She asked. On other occasions I found her on the bathroom floor and struggled to get her back to bed. Now I was able to sleep at night and our days together were so much better. Yet this prompted further feelings of guilt; my wife was in the Hospice and I was relieved.

Sarah particularly valued her time with Barbara in the Hospice. One day she was pampering her Mum, tenderly rubbing cream into her face and massaging her feet and hands. Barbara said, "Shut that door Sarah. Let it just be me and you. Nice" Those were special moments and there were, many of them in the Hospice. Paul sometimes stayed overnight in the family room so that he could spend time with his Mum. Often he would bring his keyboard so that he could play and sing to her. She loved that. One morning I arrived to find they were already in the summer house in the garden. Paul had been playing and singing some of Barbara's favourite hymns, including, 'As the deer pants for the water so my soul longs after you.' Barbara said, "I want that one for my funeral." We did sing that at her funeral a few months later and I wrote a new final verse;

When my days on earth are over

And eternity's begun;

No more pain and no more sorrow

And all my tears are done.

Then I'll bow before your throne

Make the song of heaven my own,

Freed at last at Home forever

I will truly worship You.

All the family felt those days in St. Luke's were special. One day our daughter-in-law, Katie, bathed Barbara. She didn't want a nurse or a staff member to do it that day; she wanted Katie. The ceiling of the bathroom is covered with tiny lights like a night sky; designed to be a sensory experience. It was relaxing and peaceful and Katie so valued doing that for Barbara - we all had precious memories associated with the Hospice. It was at that point, however, we were told we would have to find somewhere else for Barbara as she no longer fitted the criteria for St. Luke's. She didn't need palliative care as she wasn't in significant pain and she wasn't at the point of needing 'end of life' care. I would like to have had her home again and with help it could have been arranged, but now the other issue looming on the horizon - my own cancer and imminent operation. Our only other option was a nursing home.

We found one that had a good reputation and Sarah and I chose a room for her. She was transported to the nursing home in the Hospice vehicle, accompanied by a nurse. I went ahead so that I could get her room ready and hang family photographs on the walls. When the vehicle arrived, she refused to get out. Quite adamant, "I'm not going in there," she said and refused to move - adding brokenly, "I thought I was going home." I fought back the tears as I coaxed her inside. Once she saw the family photographs on the walls of her room her face lit and she pointed and said, "Oh." Surrounded by all the faces she loved all was well. All was well, that is, except in my heart where broken words re-echoed, "I thought I was going home."

The feeling of guilt for the bereaved usually has no rational foundation; it is a visceral response. Barbara always thought I would be the first to die. As we approached retirement, she asked me to show all our Direct Debits; what bills needed paying and who she should inform in the event of my death. The fact that she died and I survived gave me a sense of 'survivors guilt.' Laying flowers of her memorial in Ulley Church Yard always seems strange. 'You have gone and I'm still here – that was never supposed to be the deal.'

A friend told me of her feelings of guilt after her husband's death. She said, 'sins of omission' made her feel most guilty. Looking back, she was affected by things she failed to do for her husband before he died. When she had told her daughter she had exclaimed, "Oh Mum, you always went the extra mile for Dad, and then some." That helped: it is important to let yourself off the hook - when your heart is wracked by grief, be kind to yourself. I have always loved the hymn of George Matheson: 'O Love that will not let me go, I rest my weary soul in Thee.' Even in the darkest moment, I was conscious of being held by the love that will not let go. There is no better place to rest your weary soul than being loved unconditionally by the God whose Love leads you out of the dead end street of guilt.

Whilst in the nursing home one day one of the regular carers came into the room, pointed at Barbara in a picture on the wall and said, "Who is that?" "That's my Mum." Sarah had replied. "Oh wasn't she lovely," was the response. "She still is!" said Sarah. She was tearful as she recounted the incident to me. "They don't know her Dad," said Sarah. In the Nursing Home they were loud and jokey, they thought that created a friendly atmosphere but it sometimes became a stressful for one so ill as my Barbs. "They don't know her Dad."

Barbara returned to the Hospice for 'end of life care; it was like coming home. It was a relief for us to see her return to the Hospice where they really knew her and where they cared for her as a person, not just a patient. In St. Luke's they treat the whole person, body, mind and spirit. The care they gave to Barbs reminded by of the words of St. Paul from 1 Thess. 2:7 'But we were gentle among you even as a nurse cherisheth her children.' In the nursing home Barbara had switched off and turned her face to the wall. I felt she was saying 'enough.' When she returned to the Hospice she was all smiles. She recognised her nurses and carers and was so pleased to see them again. She was back for 'end of life care' and her last few days were filled with peace and kindness.

CHAPTER 9

Not Defeated

Christopher Reid writes of his own wife's death in an anthology of poems called 'The Scattering.' He writes very movingly. It was also a brain tumour that took her away from him.

He writes:

No imp or devil

but a mere tumour

squatted on her brain.

Without personality or ill humour,

Malignant but not malign,

It set about doing –

not evil,

simply the job tumours have always done:

establishing faulty

connections, skewing

perceptions, closing down

faculties and functions

One by one.

Hobgoblin, nor foul fiend;

nor even the jobsworth slob

with a slow, sly scheme to rob

my darling of her mind

that I imagined;

just a tumour.

Between which and the neat

gadget with the timer

that eased drugs into her vein,

she contrived too maintain

her identity

unimpaired and complete,

resolved to meet

death with gallantry

and distinction.

I find those lines perceptive and revealing. The ravages of cancer can have so much of the 'battle' about it. It is an unequal battle and death can feel like the final defeat. However, as I said in an earlier chapter, I could not bring myself to speak of Barbara being defeated by cancer. She remained undefeated as she moved towards death and through death. Christopher Reid's words about his wife are true of Barbara too, she 'met death with gallantry and distinction.'

Barbs never lost her humour, her connectedness, her humanity or dignity. It often surprised me that as her life narrowed she contrived to make it as wide as her undefeated personality. She came to a point when she really didn't want to see people. Meeting death with 'gallantry and distinction' meant not strenuously hanging on to life. She was letting go on her own terms. One day a colleague called to see her at the Hospice. She was pleased to see her but not overjoyed. Her colleague mentioned that her husband was waiting in the car with their little Granddaughter. She added "would you like me to ask him to bring the baby in to see you." Barbara, smiling, firmly declined the offer. She said to me afterwards, "I know people are enjoying life and have so much to live for but not me. I'm waiting to die and I want to be left to do that the best way I can." She said to people, "Don't come. Just go and get on with your own life." When one day Sarah could not hold back her tears Barbara said, "It's not your sorry Sarah." I think she would have said that to friends and family too, "It's not your sorry! Life is for living, go and do it."

There was laughter too. One day when I arrived at the nursing home Barbara was struggling to take her tights off. She had put weight on because of the strong steroids and the tights were cutting into her. I tried to help her and we got into a terrible tangle. She couldn't help herself; her legs were terribly wasted and her strength was gone; she couldn't really help me to help her. I was clumsy and inept and we became a tangle of arms and legs until we both collapsed into helpless laughter. We realised at that point that we were ideally placed for a cuddle – which we did; a long, lingering and loving cuddle. That is one of the good moments that live in my memory.

When Martin Sheen was on Desert Island Discs Kirsty Young asked him what part he had played, or film he had starred in, would he wish to be remembered. He replied that he didn't expect to be remembered for any particular part or film but for moments. He said that when people spoke to him they often said, "I remember you in..." and they would describe a scene, a moment that had left a deep impression on them. "We remember moments," he said, "life is made up of moments."

That was true of Barbara's diminishing days. There are precious moments that I revisit; cherished moments of love and inspiration that continue to breathe life and love. I thank God for them.

As Barbara approached the end speech was all but gone. We had a life time habit of holding hands and twirling each other's wedding rings. As I sat by her bed and held her hand I was reassured by the familiar twirling of my ring and I of hers. A silent communication of love. I now wear her ring on a chain around my neck and find it strangely comforting to hold and to remember the dear finger it once encircled.

I wrote in my diary on July 1st 2016, "Barbs is still trying to speak but is really incoherent." Her voice was now so quiet and even with my ear right next to her month I could not identify any words. Yet there was a kind of dialogue taking place, as if she was holding a conversation and there was animation on her face and the brightness of her personality was still present. It was strange to witness. I couldn't help but think how lively and lovely she looked despite the approach of death. She kissed my hand and I stoked her hair.

One week before Barbara died, Sunday 3rd July Sarah spent the whole of that afternoon with her Mum. I wrote about it in my diary, 'Sarah was so lovely with her Mum this afternoon. No words now but Sarah rested her head on her shoulder and Barbara held her head in place. When Sarah seemed to be lifting her head Barbs held on. It was a loving interchange between Mother and daughter.'

I have been part of St `Luke's bereavement group for a while now. I started to attend a few months after Barbara's death. It is a mutually supportive experience. One common experience, confirmed by others whose spouses have died, is that, in time the edges of grief become less jagged and the memories of moments become all the more precious and nurturing. I have found that's to be so.

On Sunday July 10th I was preaching and celebrating Holy Communion at St Oswald's Church Sheffield and then drove straight to the Hospice. Sarah was already there and Paul and Katie and the boys arrived soon after. My Sister, Edith and her husband David came in the afternoon. I wrote in my diary that day, "Barbara's breathing more laboured. Tonight I slept in her room and Paul slept in the family room at the Hospice. Her breathing became increasingly rattling. At 2.15am the nurses came into the room to turn her and make her more comfortable. At 2.30 my darling breathed her last breath and became still." The silence was palpable. A deep stillness pervaded the room. She was gone. Suddenly and irrevocably her spirit had left. Her earthly life was over. I wrote, "She is at peace at last. What an awful eighteen months she has had. She has been constantly brave and strong – never self pitying. I love you so much. Goodbye my Darling."

Within 30 minutes of her death Paul, Sarah and I stood around her bed. We held hands and I prayed a prayer, "Thank you God for a wonderful wife and Mother. Thank you for the unconditional love that she gave us and thank you for her strength that inspired us. We love her so much and commend her to your care." We wept and hugged each other and said our own goodbyes.

She lived life to the full. She extracted the nectar from the bloom of life. She lived fully and died bravely. She met death with 'gallantry and distinction.'

CHAPTER 10

Not Second Best

Before we were married Barbara and I discussed children. We talked about how many we might have. We agreed that two would be good for us, preferably a boy and a girl. We talked about what names we might give them. We also discussed our hopes and wishes for them. We broached the subject of 'what if we can't have our own children?' We both said, in unison, "We'll adopt children." It wasn't just a random thought; we discussed it thoroughly and it became a settled decision - our plan B.

We had been married for two years when we decided that this was the right time to try for a baby. Nothing happened. Eighteen months later there was still no sign of a baby. Medical investigation seemed sensible. Barbara was referred to a fertility clinic and investigation revealed problems that diminished, but did not eliminate, her chances of conception. Barbara's gynaecologist was very attentive and thorough. We lived in North Wales but he referred us to Sheffield which was one of the foremost fertility treatment centres in the country.

One of the things we had to do was to collect every drop of Barbara's urine for a whole month in plastic containers and transport it, in the boot of our car, to

Jessops Hospital in Sheffield. It felt very bizarre to be driving over the Pennines with a boot full of pee! It was surreal. A month of urine is a whole lot of liquid! We laughed about the prospect of explaining to police the contents of our boot.

At a subsequent appointment in North Wales the Consultant said to me, "We'd better get you checked too." Tests revealed that I had a low sperm count. Again this diminished but did not eliminate my chances of Fatherhood. He said he knew men whose sperm count was lower than mine but who were proud Fathers. "Both your problems added together lessen your chances of parenthood." Barbs and I were a great match in every way except for procreation, that was proving very elusive.

I was examined to determine the cause of my low sperm count and it was considered that I had a varicocele; varicose veins in the scrotum. The Doctor booked me in for surgery and said that it could significantly improve my sperm count. I came round from the anaesthetic in the Royal Alexandra Hospital, Rhyl - Barbara was by my bed. I remember being in pain and feeling ill so I said, "just leave me for now and I'll see you tomorrow." She told me later that she walked up and down Rhyl sea front, weeping.

As the days went by, however, we began to feel hopeful. Before our next appointment Barbara became convinced that she was pregnant. Her period was very late. Every day she seemed to have more symptoms of early pregnancy. She was radiant; was convinced that my operation had been a game changer. The day of our appointment she declared, "I'm pregnant Ian, I know it. I feel different. My body feels different. I'm sure we'll have it confirmed today when we see the Consultant."

We were in the waiting room when Barbs needed to visit the loo. She came back a short while later in floods of tears. She whispered hoarsely, "My period has started Ian." At that moment we were called through to the Consultant. Barbs had no time to compose herself. She sobbed broken heartedly as we sat facing our Fertility Specialist. No words could console her.

Following tests on my sperm count the news wasn't good; far from improving my chances the operation had effectively destroyed them. I received a letter of apology from the Consultant who we had seen regularly. 'I write to apologise as it is clear that your surgery, far from helping has actually resulted in a very serious reduction of your sperm count.' It was depressing news. On the strength of the letter we could have taken legal action; it was an admission of culpability. Legal action, however, would not have produced a child so all our energies transferred to the prospect of adoption. There was a growing feeling of, 'This is the way for us; this is God's plan for our family.' - we began the process of application immediately. Plan B had come into its own.

Before many months had passed Barbara and I were sitting in Office of the Chief Executive Officer of the Mission of Hope for Children's Aid and Adoption. It is an unwieldy title but came into being because of the amalgamation of two Christian Adoption Societies. He was quite an elderly clergyman and, to us, he seemed very formal. In the course of the interview he asked, "Tell me honestly, what is your view of adoption?" Without hesitation, Barbara answered "We don't regard it as second best," she said. He became suddenly animated. He leaned across his desk towards us and said, "O yes, it is second best. You wouldn't be here today if you were able to conceive naturally." Barbara thought for a moment and replied slowly and deliberately, "Well it may be plan B but plan B is no less important than plan A. It's just different - but we will love and protect our adopted children just as unreservedly as we would love our biological children." He looked at her across the wide expanse of his desk and after a pause said, "Mrs Jennings I'm sure you would fight like a tigress for your children, whether you gave birth to them or adopted them." He got that right.

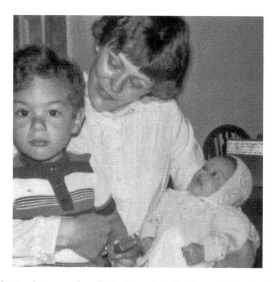

The first photograph of Barbs with Paul and Sarah. 16th July 1981, collecting Sarah.

I don't think that adoption is ever an entirely easy process; there are hurdles along the way. After being accepted we had a two year wait that seemed interminable and there were stresses and anxieties to deal with. Still the day finally came when our little family was complete with two beautiful mixed-race children. They filled our lives with love. I have a memory of walking along the promenade at Prestatyn with Barbara pushing a double buggy and her saying, "I don't need anything else Ian. I don't need foreign holidays or cars or any material thing. Everything I want is right here; our children; each other; our home; the beauty of our surroundings – who could ask for more!" She always had the capacity to live in the moment and there were some great moments. It was never second best.

Both of our children spoke at Barbara's funeral. Sarah recounted a moment in St Luke's Hospice when a doctor popped her head around the door. Sarah was sitting, shoes off, with her feet up on her Mum's bed and they were enjoying some close and cosy moments together. The doctor said, "Hello, how do you know Barbara?" Sarah gestured with open hands and said, "She's my Mum!" As if it should be perfectly obvious. Then she had the thought, "Of course it's not obvious, we're not the same colour." When you live with that difference all your life you really become unconscious of it.

Sarah went on to quote a little poem by Fleur Conklin Heyliger that Barbara had given her when she was small and it had always meant a lot to her:

> Not flesh of my flesh,
>
> Nor bone of my bone,
>
> But still miraculously my own.
>
> Never forget for a single minute,
>
> You didn't grow under my heart
>
> But in it.

Sarah kept her emotions under control and delivered her loving tribute to her Mums memory beautifully.

Paul followed her with his own tribute and he gave me permission to use that here. He said:

My Mum, Barbara Jennings, was a wife, a sister, a teacher, a grandmother, a friend, a colleague, an aunt. She was many things to many people, but to me, she was Mum. She was a devoted, caring Mother. At 5 feet two she was physically small, but the amount of love she showed us as kids and as adults, was huge. She felt all our ups and downs with us. When something good happened she was elated, and when bad stuff happened she felt every blow with us.

A couple of years ago Katie and I were living in Texas and had been trying for a baby. We'd gone down a medical pathway to get pregnant but unfortunately the pregnancy didn't turn out the way we'd hoped. When I told Mum on the phone she really felt it. She was in tears. She wanted to fly immediately out to Texas, even though we were set to return to the UK for good only 3 weeks later. She wanted to be there with us; to be a Mother to me in my moment of need.

She liked to organise her kids. She was a really organised person, which is probably why I'm so disorganised now – relied on Mum too much growing up. Mum was early every morning. Ridiculously early! Mum taught at Wales High School which I also attended along with my sister. We were always the first to arrive. Our car would pull up into an empty car park, often in the pitch black, often at 6am. Two and a half hours later the other kids would start trickling in.

A few years ago I was living in London, we went on a holiday to France and my parents came with us. I was in charge of the plan of getting us there. We went by road and had to be at Dover at 2pm for our crossing. I wanted Mum to know I'd gone above and beyond in my planning to ensure that we got there by 2pm. So I said to her, "Mum the Ferry leaves at 2pm but we have to be there by 1pm but let's add an hour to that and make it midday. Then to get from the M25 to Dover is about an hour, so that's 11am, but we'll add another hour in there so let's say 10am. It takes an hour to get round the M25, worst case, so that's 9am but add an hour in there too so that's 8am. If we add in 1 more hour for good measure that leaves us with 4 hours of wriggle room in what should only be a 2 hour journey. So we'll leave at 7am. She said, "Make it 6." No winning!

She was a proud Mum, very proud of her kids. Proud of what Sarah had achieved in Nursing and proud that I'm in the military. Only a couple of months ago, I had left work early and drove straight down to Sheffield to stay at the Hospice with Mum. I arrived still in uniform and walked into her room. I took my bag into the bathroom and she said, "where you going?" She'd lost quite a bit of cognitive ability by this point, and not everything made sense, but this was a very direct question. I said, "I'm getting changed into jeans and a T shirt Mum." She just pointed to a chair by her bed and said, "Sit." So I did as I was told and sat down. Then she didn't say anything else for the next 20 minutes or so until a nurse came in. She immediately smiled, pointed at me and said, "that's my son."

She lived life to the fullest. Whether it was walking, running, swimming, days out in York or visiting her kids, she NEVER wasted a day. She never had a lazy day or a lie in. She was up at the crack of dawn at the weekends ready to do the things she enjoyed doing. That's one thing I've learned from her. You don't have to be back packing in the Himalayas or skydiving regularly to be living life to the max, you simply have to make time to do the things you want to do; the things that make you happy. And she certainly did that.

She was also a very protective Mum. But of course as we got older, her ability to protect us and keep us safe decreased, and that made her somewhat vulnerable. When I passed my driving test I would borrow Mum and Dad's Peugeot 205 when I was in the 6th form and then later when I was home for weekends from University. Every time I went out in the car, whether I came back at 10pm or 3am, I would see Mums head and shoulders peering out of the bedroom window, anxious to know that I had returned safely. I used to ask her, "Why are you so paranoid Mum? You really don't need to worry. I've passed my driving test. Chill out!!"

She said, "You'll understand one day Paul. When you've got kids of your own you'll understand that you just can't rest until you know your kids are safe." And now, finally she rests. Her kids are safe and owe her a huge debt of gratitude. And I have Joseph and Jamie to care for and realise she was absolutely right. I hope to be the kind of parent that my parents have been to me. I know if I can come close to caring for my children as my Mum cared for me I'll have done a good job.

As I listened to our children speak so movingly about Barbara that day in her funeral service it made me realise afresh, echoing Barbara's own words, "Not second best." Never second best. Not for a moment.

The last photograph taken together of Sarah, Barbs and Paul. 25th February 2016 at St Luke's

CHAPTER 11

Only a Horizon.

I was rather surprised to discover that the line, 'All that matters is to be at one with the living God,' is from D. H. Lawrence, quoted by Richard Harries in his book, 'The Beauty and the Horror.' It is a statement that clearly expresses the foundational conviction of the Christian faith. Relationship with the God who is Love does not remove the pain and heart ache of loss, but gives you a sense of a meta narrative in which you are not alone. Excluding God from your world leaves you ultimately in a deeply lonely world. As A. E. Housman put it, 'a stranger, alone and afraid in a world I never made.'

I was heart broken after Barbara's death but I was never 'alone or afraid.'

As a Pastor I have sat with bereaved folks offering comfort and understanding. At least I thought I understood but it is not until you have experienced it yourself that full understanding dawns. I didn't know about the all-consuming sense of loss, nor did I know about the physical ache in the middle of your chest. I didn't know about the desolation and depression either. After Barbara's death I became much more sensitised to everything; I'd find myself in tears at a sad story on the TV news. I remember hugging an addict begging on the street, moved by the sight of a human being whose potential had been so comprehensively destroyed by an addictive life style. He was at the lowest ebb that a human being can reach and yet here was a person loved by God and precious in his sight. We cried together. I prayed for him too.

In my own journey of grief I kept returning to the words of St. Paul at the end of Romans Chapter eight. He asks the question, 'What can separate us from the love of Christ?' He piles up the metaphors in his exploration of what might drive a wedge of separation between us and God's love. He comes to this conclusion, 'I am convinced that nothing in death or life... nothing in all creation can separate from the love of God in Christ Jesus our Lord.' (Romans 8: 38 – 39) The eternal God has revealed himself to us in Jesus.

I remember when I was a schoolboy, my friend Peter took pride in being an atheist. It was shortly after Yuri Gagarin's space flight in 1961 when he was reported to have said, "I see no God up here." Peter quoted him, triumphantly, as if that was proof positive for the non-existence of God. I pointed into the sky and said, "Where does that end Peter?" "End?" he replied, "it doesn't end, there is no end to space." My response was, "Well, my friend, there's plenty of room for God, isn't there?"

That can seem like a cold and distant picture of God. The God who inhabits space is remote from my little life – but Jesus isn't. God in Jesus Christ is the one who forgives me, holds me, and is with me even in death and beyond death. Christian faith asserts that there is a wise and loving power behind the universe, in Jesus that power takes on personality; God is made accessible to us in Jesus.

The concept of the endless ages of eternity stretching out through infinite eons is troubling and perhaps frightening. However St. John in his Gospel gives us another picture of eternal life altogether. His emphasis is on relationship rather than duration. John 17:3 says *And this is the real and eternal life: that they may know you, the one and only true God, And, Jesus Christ whom you sent.* (The Message Bible) Here is closeness and friendship not merely knowledge about - but intimate acquaintance with.

Some people find the conventional concept of Heaven very unappealing. Hardly surprising when cartoonists often depict Heaven as a vast expanse of emptiness dotted with little fleecy clouds, occupied by floaty, ethereal beings who strum harps and look bored. That is a very tedious idea. Yet the biblical image of heaven is of a feast or banquet. Richard Harries writes, 'For many of us our most relaxed and enjoyable moments are over meals with friends or family. Heaven is above all social." I find that a heart warming concept and I am happy to leave it there; I imagine a great party. Of course,

Heaven is altogether different from our limited imaginings but it is a new and marvellously transfigured dimension of existence, where all tears will be wiped away.

A few weeks after Barbara's death I was walking along the street near my home feeling so broken inside; I was feeling that wracking sense of grief that is accompanied by an ache in the middle of the chest. I prayed as I walked and my prayer was, "God I need to know that my Barbs in all right now." I was thinking of all that she had been through; the misery and distress of the last eighteen months of her life. Images flashed through my mind of those desperate days. "What about now, how is she and where is she now?'

Suddenly and unexpectedly my mind was plunged into a deep reverie; a vivid day dream. In this heightened state of imagination, I had died and just arrived on the other side. I was walking through a brightly lit gateway and there was Barbara, waiting for me. She looked up at me, faced bathed in a radiantly sunny smile. "Oh Ian," she said, "It's amazing here, absolutely amazing. If only I'd known I would not have worried, not even for a moment." She took my hand and said, "Come on and I'll show you." I held her hand and she led me in.

That is all there was to it, but it was very vivid and deeply comforting. It would be easy to dismiss it as pure imagination and that would be reasonable, but just maybe it was a hint of Heaven, a little revelation of love. In any case it helped to ease the pain and since imagination is fed by faith it resonated deeply of peace and hope. The verse that sprang to mind was the words of St. Paul, "Eye has not seen, nor ear heard, neither has it entered the human heart the things that God has prepared for them that love him."

When I conduct funeral services I often say a prayer that I love. It has been said at very many funerals down through the years including The Queen Mother's funeral. It so well sums up the central truths of the Christian faith with regard to death:

We give our loved ones back to you O God.

Just as you first gave them to us and did not lose them in the giving, so we have not lost them in returning them to you. For life is immortal, love is eternal and death is only a horizon - a horizon is nothing but the limit of our earthly sight.

Lift us up, strong Son of God, that we may see further. Cleanse our eyes that we may see more clearly. Draw us closer to yourself that we know ourselves to be nearer to our loved ones who are with you.

'Death is only a horizon.' There is something so exciting about horizons. They beckon us to adventure. When I was a young minister in North Wales I used to visit an elderly member of my congregation called Peggy Curry.

She told me that as a little girl her family lived in Stoke on Trent. Every summer her family came on holiday to Llandudno, three of them, Mum and Dad and little Peggy. The mode of transport was motor bike and sidecar. Each year they climbed up the hill from Penryhn Bay and as the motor bike crested its brow, the full glory of the vista could be seen: the sweep of the Llandudno Bay; the grandeur of the pier and the rugged splendour of the great Orme. Their excitement was palpable - little Peggy shrieked with joy and her Dad took off his flat cap and threw it high in the air as a gesture of joyous celebration. Then he had to stop the motor bike and walk back to collect it. Peggy loved that moment and it still lived with her in old age. He did in every year.

Death is only a horizon. I have an image of throwing my cap high in the air in celebration, as that view of unimaginable splendour comes into sight beyond the final horizon.

CHAPTER 12

Grief – Pain and Process

When I sent a message of condolence to Barb Hobe following the death of her husband Hal, in 2014, she replied, "I cannot cry enough to get this deep grief from out of my heart, which is so broken." I remembered that sentence and when Barbara died it seemed to describe my own feelings so well. When tears are dried grief remains.

My son, Paul is a Wing Commander in the Royal Air Force. For a period of six years he was seconded to the American Air Force, three years in Georgia and three years in Texas. The accommodation for the family was provided by the British Embassy and was outstanding; they had not been used to a home with three bathrooms! Their temporary home was very spacious and comfortable. The two boys, Joe and Jamie had their own room, walk-in wardrobe, bathroom and lounge, where they played their games and did their homework (in theory!) so they had loads of space. When they were moving back to the UK nine year-old Jamie asked his Mum this question, "Mum how many rooms will Joe and I have in our new house?" His Mum's reply shocked him, "Only one," his eyes brows were raised in surprise, "Only one!" he echoed, questioningly. "But we will have our own bathroom won't we?" "No," was the reply. "There will be one bathroom for the whole house." His eyes brows raised further and he held out his hands palms upward, "But," he said, gesturing with empty hands, "How are we going to live?" Mum assured him that they would live quite satisfactorily and that life would be good. And so it was.

The question, "How are we going to live," is a much more serious question for many; A very real question and there are no easy answers. "How am I going to live with this agonising sense of loss?" "How am I going to live without the one I loved and with whom I shared my life?" "How am I going to live with this insupportable burden of grief?" "How am I going to live through these dark and difficult days that stretch out endlessly before me?"

They were my questions after Barbara died and it is the question that so many ask themselves at the graveside of their loved one. "How am I going to live."And yet, somehow we do live. Life is changed and will never be the same again but it is still life, a new reality to adjust to and that adjustment is a process that takes time. I know Barbara would want me to embrace life and would be cross with me if I sunk under the weight of grief. My friend's neighbour is doing just that. His wife died three years ago and yet he visits her grave daily, spending hours there. It is, sadly, the focus of his whole life and he says to my friend, "I just want to be with her." That is so sad. I often read outpourings of grief on a website for Bereaved Spouses. But someone, who is further along the same road, will come in with helpful comments about coping strategies and accessing help through counselling or attending groups or getting with friends who understand. They are finding their own answers to the question, "How am I going to live?" and they are constructing a life; maybe a life diminished but not destroyed; a different life but still a life.

Two weeks after Barbara died I sent a text to Barb Hobe saying, "Hi Barb. I have comforted many grieving people throughout the years of my ministry but living through it is truly devastating. I have lived this week on the edge of desperation. I just wondered if you had any advice or coping strategies to offer?" She replied, "Ian, I kept telling myself for the first 6 months after Hal died to get through each day. I just kept putting one foot in front of the other, cried, tried to be with others, cried, breathed, cried, and repeat. I had the disadvantage of needing to exit my house of 30 years – to downsize. I was very mad at Hal for dying and leaving me with all the stuff to sort through. Of course, that was normal and therapeutic. Intense grief, Ian, is absolutely horrible. You and I are blessed with loving children and grandchildren, and I found myself clinging to an unknown future by planning time with them. Through others I knew the comforting presence of God, who seemed a little distant. That has past, as has much of the devastation. After 41 years of being with Hal, life is very different. I am trying to model an effective grief process for my family and friends, which Hal would want. Please keep open to safe people, cherish the memories and know that you are so blessed to have shared those decades with Barbs." I found those words helpful in those days of crisis.

In 2 Corinthians 4:9 St. Paul speaks of being, "Struck down but not destroyed." He goes on to say, "so we're not giving up. How could we? Even though on the outside it often looks like things are falling apart, on the inside, where God is making new life, not a day goes by without his unfolding grace." (2 Corinthians 4:16 Message Bible.)

Western culture allows an arbitrary grieving process of two years. The message is, "it's been two years, get over it. You're fixed now – move on!" It seems to be a bit of superficial western wisdom; certainly not universal. There is a deep need in the human heart, however, not only to retain the memory of our loved one but to nurture that memory: to speak of them often; to include them in life's conversations and experiences; to hold them in love. There is no time limit on that because there is no time limit on love.

My friend, Joan Craven, was widowed in her late 40s. Her husband, Alan, had died also of brain cancer. She is a strong person and her primary concern was for her 14 year-old daughter's welfare. She was an outstanding deputy head of a primary school and she continued with her demanding job and cared for her daughter – heart broken, but functioning. They were there for each other. Life goes on. Recently, 18 years after Alan's death, Joan was invited to the 70th birthday party of a close friend. Her primary feeling at the party, however, was the pain of loss. She was surrounded by friends but felt a sense of being alone because of the absence of Alan. These were their friends; couples with whom Joan and Alan shared their younger lives. Her uppermost thought was what might have been. 18 years later and she still experienced the deep pain of loss. Joan's experience reminded me of the little poem by Elizabeth Jennings:

Time does not heal,

It makes a half stitched scar

That can be broken and you feel

Grief as total as in the first hour.

Jamie Anderson writes, 'Grief, I've learned is really just love. It's all the love you want to give, but cannot. All that unspent love gathers up in the corners of your eyes, the lump in your throat, and in the hollow part of your chest. Grief is just love with no place to go.'

Since love does not die; grief remains. It resurfaces at times when you least expect it. My friend Lyn, whose husband Ray died of cancer, calls it being, 'ambushed by grief.' After we knew her condition was terminal Barbs said to me, "You must write about this." That was her instinctive wisdom coming into play. I believe it was out of concern for my welfare. She knew that writing would make me face my grief; confronting the reality of pain and loss. I'm sure she saw that this would have therapeutic value for me - and indeed she was right. I think she also sensed that it may be a help to others, which I sincerely hope that it is. I have written most of this in the companionable atmosphere of my local café where they make the finest flat white in Sheffield! Writing in the isolation of my own apartment was just too painful at times as memories came flooding back. I have shed silent, unobtrusive tears in Café#9.

Confronting your own grief head on does contribute to an easing of the agony and memories which, at first, are painful but which become increasingly precious. It helps to talk about your loved one. All bereaved people to whom I have spoken to have this in common; they want to include their loved one in ongoing conversation with friends and family. Some people after initially expressing sympathy to a bereaved friend for the death of their loved one, then choose to keep silent perhaps because they think the person may be upset by referring to the one who has died. The contrary is true, however, it is the silence that is upsetting; it feels like a denial of their existence.

Henry James in his preface to *The Altar of the Dead* is indignant about this culture of silence which he calls, 'the awful doom of general dehumanisation.' Christopher Reid in his book of poems *A Scattering* quotes James in a poem called *Exasperated Piety*. He is writing about his own wife and says, those who have died 'are not so much forgotten as denied.' He goes on;

'I have met the tribal will,

to impose taboos and codes,

and have behaved rudely,

invoking my dead wife in dinner table conversation.'

I often 'invoke my dead wife' and our friends, perhaps taking their cue from me, speak so naturally of her remembering her quirkiness, her laughter and liveliness; I really like that.

The sub title of this little book is *Growing through Grief.* Grief without growth is a tragedy. No dark and difficult experience should be wasted: there is nurture to be received; is growth and progress to be experienced. To expand the capacity of the heart; to develop a deeper humanity; to place a renewed value on the gift of life - these are some of the possibilities of this difficult journey.

Zoe Clarke-Coates set up sayinggoodbye.org after losing five babies through miscarriage. Out of her heart ache has come hope and reaffirmation of life for so many others who deal with this so devastating experience. She writes,

Because I have cried so many tears, I now laugh more. Because I have known such sadness, I now feel great joy. Pain and loss teaches us more than anything else in life. And you know those deep valleys in your soul, that were dug by the journey of grief and sorrow? These can now be filled with happiness – you have an increased capacity for joy.

Perhaps those who have trod the deep valleys of sorrow have the potential to ascend the great heights of joy but, I don't think that Zoe Clark-Coates intended to create the idea that deep valleys of grief can be permanently replaced by high mountains of joy but rather the experience of grief expands your capacity to experience joy and there are moments when the clouds lift and the light shines with the purest radiance.

Edith Sitwell writes in her poem Eurydice;

Love is not changed by Death,

And nothing is lost and all in the end is harvest.

Agnes Whitaker commenting on those words writes, "In one sense everything is lost when someone close to you dies – close love or affection, companionship, security and many other precious needs. And yet, if 'nothing is lost' is taken to mean that no experience ultimately goes to waste, if you make use of it, it is a profound truth. .. the sorrow and anger and the guilt can often in time be turned to good account.'

Zoe Clarke-Coates is right, *'Pain and loss teaches us more than anything else in life,'* that is the key to 'Growing through grief.' For, 'not a day goes by without his unfolding grace.'

CHAPTER 13

Life after loss.

Moving from a spacious Rectory to a comparatively small apartment involved some serious down-sizing. Barbara was always up for that; she loved to throw out clutter. We often did not agree about what was rubbish to be disposed of and what was useful and needed to be kept. Barbara loved to order a skip and ruthlessly cull our belongings. This conversation was quite a frequent occurrence – Barbara; "I'm going to order a skip." Me; "We don't need a skip we haven't got enough to fill it." Barbara; "I'll fill it, just watch me!" So when it came to preparing for retirement she was in her element. Bags after bags were taken to our charity shops, operators of our local tip became like family - our Rectory became an increasingly empty space.

One thing we did agree about was what to do about our letters. During our student days we had written to each other daily – no texting in those far off days, only landlines. To talk on the phone involved arranging a day and time, and then waiting, usually by a designated phone box. Also it was expensive, whereas writing letters really was not. Three old pence was the cost of a first class letter so you could send 80 letters for one pound. It was efficient too so, we usually received each other's letters the following day. The end result, however, was a big box full of letters. Barbara tied these up with ribbon and we stored them away, moving them from loft to loft as we moved house. They were full of outpourings of undying love and expressions of affectionate endearment. So we decided what to do with them. We didn't have the luxury of storage, and besides, we didn't want to leave them gathering dust and then for our children to have to deal with them when we were gone.

We decided on a little ceremony in the Rectory garden; first thing was to buy a really good bottle of champagne, then on the appointed afternoon, lighting a fire in the garden and reading out selections of our letters to one another. Each one we read and then thrown ceremoniously on the fire. We drank a toast to our 45 year love story and we drank a toast to growing old together. It was really a celebration of love and by the end of the afternoon all the letters were burned and all the champagne was gone. It was our way of celebrating the past and anticipating the future. Two weeks later Barbara was telling my sister what we had done, when she suddenly burst into tears. "I don't know why I am crying. It was the right thing for us to do. I have no regrets and we had such a lovely afternoon, so I can't explain the tears." I understood the tears, however, it had been a moment of mourning. We had said 'Goodbye' to our younger selves in the flames of that fire and turned towards the final stages of our journey. Of course we had no way of knowing how little of Barbara's journey remained. Now that she has gone I have caught myself wishing I still had her letters, yet I know it is not what I keep in a box tied with satin ribbon that matters but what I carry in my heart.

That is true of bereavement; what we carry in our hearts sustains and inspires us.

Barbara embracing life in North Wales

We sometimes have a warped idea of courage which involves being a silent, strong, superhero, trying to ignore our pain and endeavouring to function normally in spite of our inner turmoil and distress. It is not a healthy coping strategy. If we deny our pain we never learn to cope with it. Facing the pain of loss directly and honestly is uncomfortable, but in the end it is the only way. If we don't, it may cost us dearly later when we discover we are not superhero's after all, but just humans who are bewildered, afraid, hurting and alone. Face the pain! Confront the hurt! Stare directly into the leaden clouds of desolation! In so doing we will emerge the stronger, equipped to face the future, carrying in our hearts nurturing memories and healing grace. It has taken me a while to learn that lesson.

It was my friend Roger that got me into running. He was one of the students I shared a room with when we were training for the ministry. He was big; in fact, seriously overweight. Over the years his weight had increased. He would try the latest diet and experienced some success, but would slip back into his old ways and grow larger. He moved out to the USA and planted a church on Long Island - a remarkable church. Over the past 20 years he has grown a large church with a large heart like his own. However he is no longer large.

In 2004 we had a conversation about health and excess weight. He said he had been given a clean bill of health by his Doctor, but that he could not expect to remain healthy unless he changed his life style, permanently losing a substantial amount of weight. He did it with the help of Weight Watchers, eventually losing 9 stone. Part of that journey of weight-loss included a programme of fitness. He took to running. I can't quite convey the sense of astonished surprise of his close friends on this side of the Atlantic. I remember saying to Allan, another occupant of that student room, "Have you heard that Roger is running?" He said, "I've heard it, but I can't believe it. Roger running! There must be some mistake!!" But there was no mistake.

In time, Roger became a Weight Watchers leader as well as Pastoring his large and growing church with a host of programmes. Undoubtedly he has more energy now, as he heads towards 70 than he had when he was 20! I recently had the privilege of visiting and preaching in his church. It was a great joy and there are more than 60 people in his 500 strong congregation who came to faith because they first met him as their Weight Watchers leader. Roger attended Barbara's funeral. It took place on a Friday. He flew from New York on Wednesday; attended her funeral the next day, returning to New York on the Saturday ready to lead his congregation in worship on the Sunday. He is a very inspiring human being on many levels but I never thought I would be saying he inspired me to run! But he did.

I was a late starter, running my first half marathon at the age of 65. I would never have done so if it had not been for Matt and Loran. I had officiated at their wedding

and baptised their babies. I joined their little team
money for the Children's Hospital Charity. We wer(
Izzy, named after their lovely, lively little girl Isabel. They
had been through such a worrying time. They were
grateful for the care their little girl received at the
Children's Hospital - I've been running half Marathons
ever since.

After Barbara's death my commitment to running
increased. Looking back at my 2016 diary I was surprised
by the occasions when I had written, 'Ran 10 miles today
and then swam 35 lengths after a workout in the gym.' I
was into a regime of exercise at 70 that I could not have
managed at 30! There are many such entries in my diary.
Part of my strategy was to exhaust myself so that I would
go to bed completely tired, I would not then wake in the
wee small hours to be confronted by the dark desolation
of grief. Wakefulness in the lonely watches of the night
when you are grappling with grief is very difficult. I think
there was also an element of attempting to run away from
grief - not let it catch up with me. But it can't be done.
There comes a point when you must stop running and face
your grief in all the awfulness of its heart wrenching
reality. I finally did that, but I was grateful to Roger for
inspiring me to run.

I did learn to give myself time to reflect: I walked in
the woods, sat down and shed my tears, faced my loss. I
stopped running away. But I also kept busy planning

something every day to take me out of my home - to meet people and occupy my mind and my time. To even the most trivial thing but I would try to give a sense of occasion. Every Sunday morning I would preach and celebrate the Eucharist at various churches. Every Sunday morning was occupied. I valued that because of the pastoral connection and because the weekly discipline of sermon preparation that kept my heart and mind engaged. I also attended worship for my own spiritual nurture; at Endcliffe Christ Church on Sunday afternoons at 3.00 and St Marks Night Service at 8pm. Two churches that are hugely contrasting in theology and practice, but both gave me something I needed in terms of prayer focus, faith affirmation and spiritual nurture.

My children played a huge part in the process of healing. Paul was living in Harrogate and I drove each Friday afternoon to pick up Jamie from school; that was always a life affirming joy. Then we would walk to the Burger Bar and Joseph would come from his school to join us, while Paul drove straight to meet us from work. Katie was still at work and we would see her later. So it was an all boys event and a regular Friday treat. On the Saturday morning Paul, Joe and myself did Parkrun together whilst Katie would take Jamie to football practice. I can't put into words how important this weekly routine was to me.

Sarah and I talked endlessly about Barbara and there was always laughter - lots of laughter - as well as tears. A regular feature of our routine was to have breakfast together after Sarah had finished her night shift; always a lovely way to start my day. There were more special moments too. We had placed Barbara's ashes in two locations. The first is the little memorial garden in Ulley Churchyard which I had dedicated before my retirement. The second was under 'our tree' on the ridge beyond Mam Torr. Barbara loved that place. Sarah and I walk there and sometimes take a picnic. It is never a maudlin experience. One recent, glorious Bank Holiday when Sarah had missed the sunshine because she had slept all day following her night shift, she said to me, "let's walk up to Mam Torr this evening and watch the sunset." We did that and we had it all to ourselves. The silence was palpable - beauty was – soul-stirring - The light was all golden glow - it was a deeply healing moment for us both.

I had many minor coping strategies but my primary one was love. That was Barbara's legacy. She cared deeply for us and us for her. That loving care was Barbara's gift to us and we share that with one another as a family, helping us to move forward into healing. When some loved and loving member of a family dies it changes the family dynamic, leaving a huge vacuum. It is a choice to move closer together, to close the gap and let love triumph over loss.

Barbara said some interesting things even when her understanding had diminished significantly. She surprised me one day when the tumour was asserting its hold; "The time for passivity is over the time for dynamism is here." I remembered those words after her death. The dynamics of our family had changed, there was no time for passivity. The dynamic of love would sustain us on the journey of healing. That was our choice as a family; love is always the right choice.

If I could offer one word of advice to people on this journey it would be 'Say Yes to life!' Keep saying yes when the days are at their most desperate; when the darkness is closing in around you; when you are crumpled and broken keep saying 'Yes' to life. And life will say 'Yes' to you.

Twelve months after the death of Barbara I received a phone call from our son Paul. "Some good news for you Dad. Katie is expecting a baby!" It was extraordinarily good news and wholly unexpected. Three treatments of IVF resulted in nothing. Pauls eulogy at his Mums funeral spoke of her tears at the news of that disappointment and her desire to fly out to Texas to be with them. They came home to the UK and had accepted that a baby wasn't going to happen for them, had said to each other, 'Life is good – we have two wonderful boys to care for and so much to be thankful for.' They acquired two puppies, with boundless energy, and their lives seemed complete. Now suddenly, miraculously, a baby was on the way. My euphoria was tinged with sadness. Barbara would have so loved to hold this baby in her arms.

George arrived in February 2018. Needless to say he is a great blessing and a joy beyond words. I find myself talking to Barbara about him. Maybe she knows already. Maybe she is permitted to draw aside a curtain and observe from that better land. Maybe she shares in the joy and participates in our celebration. I'd like to think so. In fact some have suggested Barbara's arrival in the next world and George's arrival in this world are connected. Barbara's friend and colleague, Jude Cole said, "How she would have loved that little boy – he really is a healing gift to you all. I'm sure she had a hand in it somewhere!" Jude isn't the first to suggest that - it may be a bit of homespun theology but if the 'faithful departed' have an intercessory role, you can bet that Barbs would have been making a strong case for a baby for Paul and Katie! One thing that Jude is absolutely right about is that 'he really is a healing gift.'

I attend a church home group on Tuesday evenings. One of the things they do is to get every member of the group to write a letter to themselves at the end of the year setting out personal aspirations for the following year. The letter is sealed and kept and given back to you to open twelve months later. At the end of 2016 I wrote this to myself:

To Myself,

2016 was the worst year of my life. My lovely, lively Barbs died after a harrowing and heroic battle with brain cancer. I am grateful for a life partner who was strong, inspiring and beautiful. We were married for 44 years. I thank God for her and for two awesome children whose love and support have been beyond price during Barbara's illness and after her death. I am grateful for friends and family whose love and encouragement has always been there for me.

I am also grateful for coming through my own cancer crisis. July 4th – one week before Barbs died, I was told I was cancer- free following radical surgery. I am glad to be alive. I miss Barbs everyday but I know she would want me to get on with living.

So – plans and aspirations for 2017

- *More reading*

- *Continue exercise in preparation for half marathon and marathon.*

- *Healthy diet and some weight loss!*

- *Nurture friendships – see friends often.*

- *Be effective in ministry – prayer – study – preaching – diligent in pastoral work.*

- *Grasp opportunities*
- *Smile and laugh more!*
- *Be more tactile – warm and winsome! Not standoffish!*
- *Visit Roger and Gill – New York*
- *Visit Dave and Margaret – Australia*
- *Walk more – long distance trails.*
- *Run! Run! Run!*
- *Be as good a Dad as I can be – Paul and Sarah have lost their Mum. Maybe I can be more caring, loving, and available.*
- *Help Sarah with her allotment!*
- *Get closer to those amazing boys – Joe and Jamie.*
- *Continue to learn classical guitar.*
- *Join a mid-week walking group.*
- *Join a reading group.*
- *Write regularly – about Barbs – By a Departing Light.*
- *Drink less!*
- *Be Hospitable.*

If when I open this letter in 12 months time I have had a good, energetic crack at these aspirations I will be pleased. But whatever has or has not been achieved keep on loving yourself because God does!!

Love from Ian.

Writing your hopes and aspirations; forming your plans and writing them down are practical ways of saying 'Yes' to life. There is life after loss. Mother Julian of Norwich wrote;

He said not: thou shalt not be tempested, thou shalt not be travailed; thou shalt not be afflicted; but he said: thou shalt not be overcome.

"You will not be overcome." Through the harrowing journey of grief the message to all who say 'Yes' to life, however tentatively, is 'You will not be overcome." Say 'Yes' to life and though you may face deep troughs of desperation and heart trembling turbulence, eventually life will say 'Yes' to you.

Jesus said, 'I have come that you might have life in all its fullness.' (John 10:10) That includes those who mourn. There is life, full life, after loss.

Walking along the coast of Robin Hood's Bay, 2014

Bibliography

Blue like Jazz by Donald Miller. Thomas Nelson 2003.

Revelation of Divine Love by Mother Julian of Norwich (1395) She lived from 1342 – 1416. Her book is the first in the English language known to be written by a woman. Currently published by Paraclete Press.

God of Surprises by Gerard Hughes. Darton Longman and Todd 2015.

A Grief Observed by C S Lewis. Faber and Faber 1961 and 2015.

Connection through Compassion by Joni James Aldrich and Nysa M Peterson. Written by two women who cared for their husbands with terminal brain cancer. 2015 available through Amazon.

On Death and Dying by Elizabeth Kubler-Ross 1969 and 2008 Blackwell.

Religious Factors in the Etiology and treatment of Alcoholism. Howard Clinebell Quarterly Journal of Studies, no 24 1963.

Grenfell Hope by Gaby Doherty 2018 SPCK

A Scattering by Christopher Reid Arête Book 2009.

The Beauty and the Horror by Richard Harries SPCK 2018

The Altar of the of the Dead by Henry James William Heimann, London 1895

All in the end is Harvest – an anthology edited by Agnes Whitaker. Darton Longman and Todd. 1994

Saying Goodbye by Zoe Clarke-Coates. David C Clarke 2017

Reviews

The Bishop of Leicester writes:

"I had the privilege of working with Ian in Sheffield so it is no surprise to me that this deeply personal and moving account of his loss and grief is so filled with faith and confidence in God. Ian has been a pastor and teacher for many years, but his biggest challenge was learning to care for himself when the love of his life fell ill then died. This book will be invaluable for anyone facing pain and loss. It is full of rich resources for reflection and prayer. Above all, it is a reminder that when Jesus said he would be with us "always, to the end of the age," he meant it.

The Rt. Revd Martyn Snow, Bishop of Leicester.

Sue Mellor Headteacher, All Saints School, Aston

Ian's book – *'By a Departing Light'* is an honest and poignant account of his own grief on the loss of his beautiful wife, Barbara. It is a description of his own journey, sustained and surrounded by the power of God's healing love.

"Everyone's journey of grief is different." Those who lose someone close to them ask the question "How am I going to live without the one I love?" The answer for everyone is different too but Ian explains…. "It's what we carry in our hearts that sustains us and inspires us…"

At the end of the book Ian leaves the reader with a strong message, deeply rooted in Barbara's own spirit and passion for life and for those she loved – "Say yes to life and life will say yes to you." The Pain of losing someone you love never goes away but "By a Departing Light" will move you to tears and make you smile but above all will provide comfort and hope to all who read it.

The Bishop of Oxford.

Ian is a Priest of deep integrity and pastoral experience. I found it moving to read his account of Barbara's illness and this own bereavement, I warmly commend By a Departing Light.

The Rt Revd Dr Steven Croft, Bishop of Oxford.

Jude Cole writes:

> When I read this book, I am vividly reminded of the voice, face and above all, the ever present laughter that my dear friend Barbs shared with all our lives.

> Above all through the agony and grief, which her wonderful family have undergone, runs a sure, profound faith and power of enduring love as a force to heal.

Jude Cole, Wales High School.

Rev. Dr. Andrew Davies

> Deeply personal, profoundly moving desperately sad and remarkably honest, *'By a Departing Light'* tells of a family's tragedy with immense warmth, faith and ultimately, hope. Ian tells the story of loving and losing his wife Barbara with an intensity that is a fitting tribute to her and to their relationship. Those who have gone through such loss will undoubtedly find his words resonating with, and helping them confront, their own most intimate emotions, whilst those so far spared such personal tragedy will gain genuine insight into the most challenging experience that life could ever confront them with. By no means an easy read, but a remarkable one, that, whilst it brought more than

a few tears to my eye, ultimately left my heart strengthened.

Rev. Dr. Andrew Davies, Reader in the Public Understanding of Religion, Birmingham University

Printed in Great Britain
by Amazon